SO-BFC-604

fat/trax

COLORADO SPRINGS

David Crowell

FALCON   Helena, Montana

A **FALCON**GUIDE

Falcon Press is continually expanding its list of recreational guidebooks. All books include detailed descriptions, accurate maps, and all the information necessary for enjoyable trips. You can order extra copies of this book and get information and prices for other Falcon guidebooks by writing Falcon Press, P.O. Box 1718, Helena, MT 59624 or calling toll free 1-800-582-2665. Also, please ask for a free copy of our current catalog.
Our e-mail address is: falconbk@ix.netcom.com

©1996 by Falcon Press Publishing Co., Inc.,
Helena and Billings, Montana.

All rights reserved, including the right to reproduce this book or parts thereof in any form, except for inclusion of brief quotations in a review.

Printed in Canada.

Cover photo by Cheyenne Rouse.

Library of Congress Cataloging-in-Publication Data
Crowell, David, 1965-
    Fat trax : Colorado Springs / David Crowell.
        p.   cm.
    Includes index.
    ISBN 1-56044-448-7 (pbk.)
    1. All terrain cycling—Colorado—Colorado Springs—Guidebooks
    2. Colorado Springs (Colo.)—Guidebooks.   I. Title.
GV1045.5.C62C633   1996
796.6'4'0978856—dc20   96-25641
                                              CIP

CAUTION

Outdoor recreational activities are by their very nature potentially hazardous. All participants in such activities must assume the responsibility for their own actions and safety. The information contained in this guidebook cannot replace sound judgment and good decision-making skills, which help reduce the risk exposure, nor does the scope of this book allow for disclosure of all the potential hazards and risks involved in such activities.

Learn as much as possible about the outdoor recreational activities in which you participate, prepare for the unexpected, and be cautious. The reward will be a safer and more enjoyable experience.

 Text pages printed on recycled paper.

Contents

RIDES

Acknowledgments

My life has been touched by many people. All of whom helped make me who I am! A global thanks to all my friends...you are my strength. Thanks.

Matt, did you know that buying a car would set off such a chain of events? Or do you think it was something Morika slipped into the chicken? Your biking prowess has very little to do with my thanks. However, I'd probably not have written this otherwise.

Moose, thanks for showing me the way and speaking up for me when I got there.

Thanks to Jane for making my home away from home warm, cozy, and full of positive energy.

· I want to thank Sandi for many things. Yet, I don't know how. Oh, I guess I just did.

I couldn't be typing these words without Jaan. I hope I can repay you! Thanks for answering the phone back in 1988. It changed my life.

Chuck, who kept me sheltered and sane, your friendship · is truly special. Thanks for letting me in, putting me up, and putting up with me. Too bad Albert and Boomer can't read. Oh well, let 'em sniff the book.

Mummy, thanks for being you. Your happiness is inspirational and your love perfect.

Dad, thanks for showing me the world and teaching me to cope with it. Thanks too, for not making me grow up. Your love is perfect.

Clint, this is as much your book as my own. The funny thing is, I don't know why. Sure, your support and endurance made this possible. That's not it, though. Sure, your love empowers me. But, that's not it either. I guess it's just you. Being brothers is hard. Thanks for being mine.

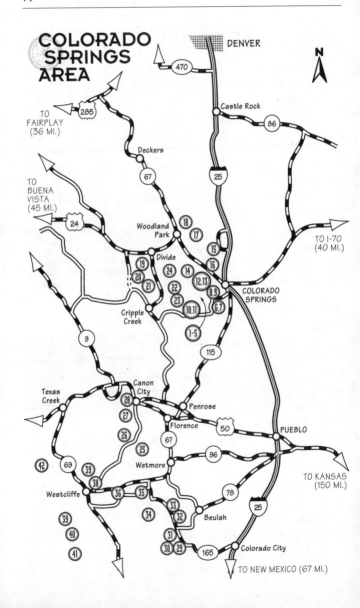

MAP LEGEND

 Trail

 Unimproved Road

 Paved Road

 Gravel Road

 Interstate

 Wilderness Boundary

 Waterway

 State Line

 Lake/Reservoir

 Cliff

 Camping

 Ruins

 Town

 City

 Trailhead

 Route Marker

 Mountain Peak (Overview map)

 Parking

 Mile Marker

 Interstate

 U.S. Highway

 State Highway

 Forest Road

 Gate

 Building

Get Ready to CRANK!

Mountain bikers, beginner to expert, all share a common need: A place to ride. *Fat Trax: Colorado Springs* gives the fat tire enthusiast the skinny on where to ride.

Now you can put variety into your mountain biking diet! The 42 rides in this book range from easy rollers to lung-busting loops. You will be able plan rides knowing what's in store. *Fat Trax* guides rate each ride for two types of difficulty: the *physical effort* required to pedal the distance, and the level of *bike-handling skills* needed to stay upright and make it home in one piece. We call these **Aerobic level** and **Technical difficulty** (the ratings are explained on pages 4 and 5).

Our aim here is three-fold: to help you choose a ride that's appropriate for your fitness and skill level; to make it easy to find the trailhead; and to help you complete the ride safely, without getting lost. Take care of these basics and fun is bound to break loose.

The Pike's Peak Region and Beyond

Fat Trax: Colorado Springs covers a lot of ground. Sixty-five miles north and south by 60 miles east and west to be precise. That's 3,900 square miles! To make the guide easy to use, the rides have been grouped into 5 geographic sections: Colorado Springs, Woodland Park - Divide, Canon City, San Isabel Lake, and Wet Mountain Valley - Sangre de Cristo Mountains.

The majority of the rides are within a 30 minute drive of Colorado Springs and the rest are reasonably close. Each section has special information pertaining to the area and additional rides that couldn't be packed in. A brief synopsis of the sections is in order.

The **Colorado Springs** area presents the core curriculum of rides with the main campus being Pike's Peak and North Cheyenne Canyon. These rides all lie within minutes of downtown and run the full gamut of abilities.

Woodland Park - Divide rides put variety in the schedule. Most of the rides are rated moderate and the scenery is incredible. The crowds here will vary, but they tend to be smaller than in Colorado Springs. Check out Mueller State Park!

If nearby solitude is what you want, **Canon City** is the region. The crowds are few and the rides are moderate to strenuous. The Tanner-Stultz loop is one of the most technically challenging in this guide.

San Isabel offers it all! The listed rides are for the hardcore. Moderate and easy rides can also be found in the region. The drive time of over an hour usually filters out casual riders. Great singletrack and challenging terrain are surrounded by unspoiled forest. Overnight camping is available as is some modest lodging. See the hand-built, medieval-style castle while in the region!

The **Wet Mountain Valley** lies about one and a half hours from Colorado Springs. Camping and modest lodging is readily available for weekend plans. The valley and the majestic **Sangre de Cristo Mountains** offer rides from easy to strenuous, good for all abilities. Lots of history here! Spanish conquistadors, German colonists, miners, and Ute Indians have all called this valley home. WARNING: Spending time here can be habit forming!

A Guide to the Guide

Most of the information in this book is self-explanatory. But if anything in a ride description doesn't seem to make sense, re-read the following explanation of our format.

The **maps** are clean, easy-to-use navigational tools. Closed trails are not usually shown on the maps but may be listed in the ride description.

The **elevation profiles** provide a good look at what's in store by graphically showing altitude change, tread, and ratings (see page 6). Out and back rides are shown only in one direction. Simply reverse the direction of travel for the return profile. The ratings listed on the profiles are defined below.

The rest of the information is listed in an "at-a-glance" fashion. It is divided into 12 sections:

The **Ride number** refers to where the ride falls in this guide. Use this number when cross-referencing between rides for an easy method of finding the descriptions. The **Ride name** refers to the most common name for the trail. Many trails in the region have been changing names faster than they can make signs. Maps might still show the old names and numbers. This shouldn't be a problem except maybe at the coffee shop.

Location tells, in general, where the ride is.

Distance gives the ride's length in miles.

Time is an *estimate* of how long it will take to complete the ride. It is *trail* time and does not include stops. If the ride is rated as more difficult or strenuous than what you usually ride, add some time to the estimate. If it's rated a lot higher, add a big chunk of time! It might take strong, skilled riders less time. Compare your ride times with those listed in the guide and adjust your estimates accordingly.

Tread describes what the tires ride on. Singletrack, dirt road, and doubletrack are common examples. A note or two will be included if conditions aren't good.

Aerobic Level *estimates* the physical challenge of the ride. The levels are: easy, moderate, and strenuous. A note here will describe any special details pertaining to the rating.

Easy rides are mostly flat, but this may include some rolling hills. Any climbs will be short.

Moderate rides will have climbs; some might be steep. Long, gradual hills also fall in this category. Strenuous sections may occur, but the majority of the ride is moderate. Even on a moderate ride, some steeper sections may force some cyclists to dismount and walk.

Strenuous rides put the granny gear to work! Not many people will ride these without walking. The steeps may be long, grueling tests of endurance, power, and determination.

Remember, these ratings are for comparison's sake. Easy rides can still have you gulping air and moderate ones may have you walking. Walking a bike is a perfectly legitimate way to transport it. Remember, this guide is for beginners to experts. Therefore, compare your first rides to the levels to get a feel for the classifications. The levels are paired with the technical ratings. Technical sections that exceed your ability are tiring and will increase the Aerobic level.

Technical difficulty is not a problem with your TV. It is a scale from 1 to 5 that quantifies how much biking skill is needed to keep the rubber-side down. Specific reasons for the rating might be listed.

Level 1: Basic bike riding skills needed. The tread is smooth and without obstacles, ruts, or steeps.

Level 2: Mostly smooth tread with minor difficulties. Ruts, loose gravel, or obstacles may exist. However, they are easily avoidable.

Level 3: Irregular tread with some rough sections, steeps, obstacles, gravel, sharp turns, or open switchbacks. These will have route options or "lines" through them.

Level 4: Rough going! The tread is uneven with few smooth sections. The line is limited as it goes through rocks, roots, branches, ruts, sidehills, narrow tread, loose gravel, and switchbacks. These obstacles often occur on steeps!

Level 5: Continuously broken, rocky, root-strewn, or trenched tread with frequent, sudden, and severe changes in gradient. Slopes necessitating off-the-seat riding and nearly continuous obstacles such as listed above exist. The line might be hard to find.

Pluses and minuses cover the in between areas.

A ride's rating describes the majority of the ride. Sections that rate higher can be found in the ride description and profile. Extreme obstacles may be listed by the main rating and in Highlights.

Again, these ratings are for comparison's sake. Riders proficient in gravel riding techniques may have an easier time on one trail than riders who rip up the switchbacks. Gauge your ability on the first few rides against the scale to get a feel for the ratings.

Highlights is where to find the ride's emotional story. Qualities that make the ride unique and specific hazards will be listed here.

Land Status: The rides in this guide are mostly on public lands. Appendix B gives the information needed to contact the various land management agencies about rules, regulations, and updates.

Maps is a list of maps that shows the ride's area. The USGS maps listed for the ride can be used for a more detailed view, and the Forest Service maps are useful in finding additional rides. They are interesting but might not show the ride's route. A glance at the topo shows the climbs and descents. But so do the elevation profiles in this guide.

Access is how to find the trailhead. The directions are from a common point in the region. Directions to that point may be found in each regional introduction. High Drive Parking lot has a page to itself (page 15) and rides using it are referred to that page.

The ride lists where to go and how to find your way back. Attached to the descriptions are odometer readings. These are *estimates*! Bike computers aren't the best measuring devices. But it should give a good idea of where things lie.

This guide doesn't pretend to be omniscient. Ratings are as accurate as possible. However, everyone is different. Individual riders seem to excel in different skills and this can affect the actual difficulty of a ride. A guide is a starting point. Every effort has been made to deliver an accurate account of the rides. Regulations, ownership, and even the land itself change. This guide should still get you home in one piece. If you have an inadvertent adventure, drop us a line.

Elevation Graphs

An elevation profile accompanies each ride description. Here the ups and downs of the route are graphed on a grid of elevation (in feet above sea level) on the left and miles pedaled across the bottom.

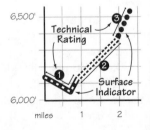

Route surface conditions (see map legend), and technical levels are shown on the graphs.

Note that these graphs are compressed (squeezed) to fit on the page. The actual slopes you will ride are not as steep as the lines drawn on the graphs (it just feels that way). Also, some extremely short dips and climbs are too small to show up on the graphs. All such abrupt changes in gradient are, however, mentioned in the mile-by-mile ride description.

Being prepared

Fat Trax: Colorado Springs is a where-to-ride book. *How* to ride is another story. However, "what to bring" lies in the grey area between the two subjects. Common sense is the rule here. Bring what makes you feel comfortable. If you need a personal mechanic to follow you, pay Bikeshop Bob to do so. If you like riding in just shorts and a hat, well, it's your body. Here are a few ideas on tools, first-aid, clothing, altitude sickness, drinking water, and weather.

TOOLS

Tools are a touchy subject for bikers; everyone has his or her own opinion. When deciding how many tools to bring, I keep one question in mind. "What's the farthest I'd have to walk?" I weigh out the tools and my desire not to walk, which usually leads to the following list.

spare tube
patch kit
allen wrench (pocket-knife style)
channel locks
air pump
spare cables (rear derailleur and rear brake)
small bit of baling wire

If you can't replace a tube without tire levers then bring them (learning the task will save weight and punctured tubes).

This list is too short for some and too much for others. If you get stranded remember that, with time, everywhere is within walking distance.

FIRST AID

A first aid kit should be considered. Prevention is the first thing to put in the kit. However, if something happens it's good to be prepared. Again, I think of one question. "How far am I from help?" Here's a partial list of things to consider.

butterfly-closure bandages
adhesive bandages
gauze compress pads and gauze wrap
allergy pills
emergency water purification tablets
moleskin
antiseptic swabs
sun screen
energy bar

The best thing in the kit is usually a riding partner. Riding alone in remote areas isn't wise. If something happens remain calm and make decisions with a clear mind. Also bear in mind the primary rule of first aid is "do no harm." This means doing only what you must to keep the injured person alive and as comfortable as possible until you can get to a doctor. For example, imagine your partner is bitten by a rattlesnake. You can both coast to the car in two minutes, and it's a short drive to the nearest town. Why waste time with a snakebite kit?

Some standard cycling apparel also makes sense from a first-aid standpoint. Wear a helmet. Gloves and cycling shorts are pretty much a given. Gloves will save your hands at one time or another and cycling shorts will save your butt. Sunglasses help prevent burned out retinas and also offer some protection from dust, kamikaze insects, and rocks spun up by the knobby in front of you.

Altitude sickness shouldn't be a problem for most locals. But visitors from lower elevations may feel its effects. Headache, nausea, dizziness, and fatigue are warning signs. Also check for irregular breathing and a rapid, bounding heart rate at rest. If these symptoms don't subside, or if any one of them is severe enough to cause distress, descend to a lower elevation immediately. These relatively mild symptoms can rapidly progress to a more serious build up of fluid in the lungs or brain, either of which can be deadly.

The best way to avoid altitude sickness is to give your body plenty of time to acclimate to higher elevations. Riders from sea level should probably take it easy the first few days in Colorado. Drink lots of water, juice, and electrolyte drinks; avoid caffeine and alcohol. Eating a healthy diet also helps. Also remember that altitude sickness is unpredictable. It can strike anyone, even the young, healthy, and physically fit. Some people suffer mild symptoms at elevations as low as 5,000 feet. And the symptoms can strike even days after a person has apparently acclimated to altitude.

WATER

The water question is twofold: "How much do I need?" and "Where can I get more?"

The human body needs a lot of water. Experts say in summer heat a person exercising hard uses 1.5 to 2.5 gallons of water each day. That's a lot of water! And higher elevations tend to increase the need. I carry two water bottles and keep a gallon jug in the car. I also us an electrolyte replacement drink-mix, like Gatorade.

For extremely long rides, a refill may be needed. Colorado's streams and lakes may look clear and clean, but you can't drink straight from them without treating the water first. The problem? A pesky little protozoan called *Giardia lamblia*. Giardia is a waterborne parasite that causes intense gastrointestinal problems. It's a bug that isn't fun to catch but is easy to avoid. *Don't drink untreated water!* Packing a purification method allows on-the-go refilling. Filters are the best way to treat backcountry water. Some cyclists like to go light and use chlorine, Halazone, or iodine tablets. These, however, are not fully reliable and may pose hazards of their own. Check with local sporting goods stores for water filters.

One other note. If creek water splashes onto a water bottle, let the bottle's water flow over the drinking spout to rinse it off before imbibing.

WEATHER

Mother Nature is a beautiful and wonderful thing. But she doesn't plan weather around bike rides. Colorado's weather is notoriously unpredictable. Rain, wind, and even snow can whip up in any season. Usually this just lends a bit of adventure to the ride. But one person's adventure may be another's worst nightmare. Just remember: panic is not a survival tool!

Thunderstorms are frequent afternoon visitors to the region. With little warning they roll in, blowing, raining, and hailing. Temperatures dip and lightning cracks. Luckily they pass quickly. When a storm starts forming it's wise to turn around and head for home. If you do get caught in the open, some precautions can help keep you safe.

Check how close the lightning is with the old trick of counting the seconds between the flash and the thunderclap. A "five-Mississippi" count is about 1 mile. If the bolts are closer than a couple of miles, it's time to take precautions. When out in the open, ditch the bike and metal objects. Then get away. Don't be the tallest thing around and do not hide under a lone tree. The idea is to avoid being a lightning-rod or hiding under it. Look for a depression or low point and crouch down. Don't lie down and do try to avoid puddles and moving water. The water or metal objects can conduct lightning. In a forest, find shelter by moving downhill and seeking out a solid stand of smaller trees. Caves and overhangs are usually a bad idea— lightning can flash across their openings or carom inside.

The odds of getting hit by lightning are quite slim. However, they are greater than the chances of winning the Lotto. Do you play Lotto?

During a storm, temperatures usually drop dramatically. Paired with rain and wind, hypothermia (lowering of your core body heat) becomes a real threat. Try to keep dry and out of the wind. Exercise and an energy bar should keep you warm, but it's not a sure thing. Dress for current and predicted conditions and be ready for unexpected changes. I bring a shell to cut the wind and rain even on sunny days. Some people toss in rain pants. High-altitude rides call for cold weather gear and possibly snow gear. Bring what makes you comfortable. Bear in mind that wet weather can make trails boggy, turning a short ride into a long (cold) one.

Most of the good off-road riding in the region around Colorado Springs and the Wet Mountain Valley happens from mid-June through October. Some trails, particularly at higher elevations, have much shorter seasons running from late July through August. (Bear in mind that hunting seasons in some areas may overlap prime pedaling times. For specific dates check with the Colorado Division of Wildlife; see Appendix B).

At any time of year rain or snow can turn trails to purée for days afterward. Please stay off wet, muddy trails. The risk of soil damage and erosion is simply too great.

In the Colorado Springs area, North Cheyenne Canyon usually dries out early and stays rideable late into fall. Rides 1, 2, 3, 6, 7, and 9 are good bets during seasonal transitions.

Woodland Park tends to get snow sooner than The Springs. However, Mueller Park has some fabulous late fall rides. Keep an eye on the weather and check out rides 19 through 21.

Rides 27 and 28 grant Canon City an almost year-round riding season.

The rides around San Isabel Lake usually offer great late-season action. While the area gets cold, the snow tends to hit later. Watch the weather, dress warmly, and then try rides 30, 32, 33, and 35.

The road rides in the Wet Mountain Valley can be ridden year-round. The occasional blizzard will shut down the fun, but only until the plows come. See rides 36, 37, and 38.

Ridin' Right!

If every mountain biker always yielded the right-of-way, stayed on the trail, avoided wet or muddy trails, never cut switchbacks, never skidded, always rode in control, showed respect for other trail users, and carried out every last scrap of what was carried in (candy wrappers and bike-part debris included)—in short, if we all *did the right thing*—we wouldn't need a list of rules governing our behavior.

Fact is, most mountain bikers are conscientious and are trying to do the right thing. Most of us own that integrity. (No one becomes good at something as demanding and painful as grunting up sheer mountainsides by cheating.)

Most of us don't need rules.

But we do need knowledge of what exactly *is* the right thing to do?

Here are some guidelines—I like to think of them as reminders—reprinted by permission from the International Mountain Bicycling Association. The basic idea is to prevent or

minimize damage to land, water, plants, and wildlife, and to avoid conflicts with other backcountry visitors and trail users. Ride with respect.

IMBA RULES OF THE TRAIL

Thousands of miles of dirt trails have been closed to mountain bicyclists. The irresponsible riding habits of a few riders have been a factor. Do your part to maintain trail access by observing the following rules of the trail, formulated by the International Mountain Bicycling Association (IMBA). IMBA's mission is to promote environmentally sound and socially responsible mountain biking.

1. Ride on open trails only. Respect trail and road closures (ask if not sure), avoid possible trespass on private land, obtain permits and authorization as may be required. Federal and state wilderness areas are closed to cycling. The way you ride will influence trail management decisions and policies.

2. Leave no trace. Be sensitive to the dirt beneath you. Even on open (legal) trails, you should not ride under conditions where you will leave evidence of your passing, such as on certain soils after a rain. Recognize different types of soil and trail construction; practice low-impact cycling. This also means staying on existing trails and not creating any new ones. Be sure to pack out at least as much as you pack in.

3. Control your bicycle! Inattention for even a second can cause problems. Obey all bicycle speed regulations and recommendations.

4. Always yield trail. Make known your approach well in advance. A friendly greeting (or bell) is considerate and works well; don't startle others. Show your respect when passing by slowing to a walking pace or stopping. Anticipate other trail users at corners and blind spots.

5. Never spook animals. All animals are startled by an unannounced approach, a sudden movement, or a loud noise. This can be dangerous for you, others, and the animals. Give animals extra room and time to adjust to you. When passing horses use special care and follow directions from the horseback riders (dismount and ask if uncertain). Running cattle and disturbing wildlife is a serious offense. Leave gates as you found them, or as marked.

6. Plan ahead. Know your equipment, your ability, and the area in which you are riding—and prepare accordingly. Be self-sufficient at all times, keep your equipment in good repair, and carry necessary supplies for changes in weather or other conditions. A well-executed trip is a satisfaction to you and not a burden or offense to others. Always wear a helmet.

Keep trails open by setting a good example of environmentally sound and socially responsible off-road cycling.

Don't let all of these precautions dampen your enthusiasm! Biking this region is great! Just pay attention to yourself, those around you, and the environment. And have fun!

Colorado Springs: High Drive Parking Lot - North Cheyenne Canyon

Many of the rides in the immediate Colorado Springs area share this common starting point. Some rides listed also mention parking elsewhere along the shoulder of High Drive. But this one-way road is open only in summer, so if you're riding here in spring or fall, park in the designated parking lot. All of the odometer readings for High Drive rides begin from the parking lot.

The rides are described individually, but they also work well when linked into various loops. Look at the map and refer to the mileages and difficulty ratings in each description, and then make up your own route.

ACCESS

Cheyenne Boulevard and Gold Camp Road both lead from Colorado Springs to this parking lot. From town, take Cheyenne Boulevard westbound. Turn right at the entrance to Seven

Falls and continue up into North Cheyenne Canyon. The pavement ends at the High Drive lot. The other option from town is to head west on U.S. Highway 24 and turn left (south) onto 21st Street. Then turn right onto Lower Gold Camp Road and go straight at the four-way stop. Drive past the Section 16 parking lot to an intersection with High Drive. Proceed up Gold Camp Road, which turns to dirt and ends in the High Drive lot.

Captain Jack's

Location: North Cheyenne Canyon Park, 5 miles west of Colorado Springs.

Distance: 5.4-mile loop.

Time: 45 minutes to 1.5 hours.

Tread: 2.5 miles of singletrack and 2.9 miles of dirt road. The downhill portion of singletrack is gravelly.

Aerobic level: Moderate. Most of the climb is in the first mile.

Technical difficulty: Mostly 2 and 3, with 0.4 mile of 3+. Gravel is the main obstacle.

Highlights: Ride this very popular singletrack in a clock-wise direction! The singletrack serves up some tight turns, gravel, and vistas of the canyon and city. Watch out for motorcycles on the singletrack of this good lunch-hour choice.

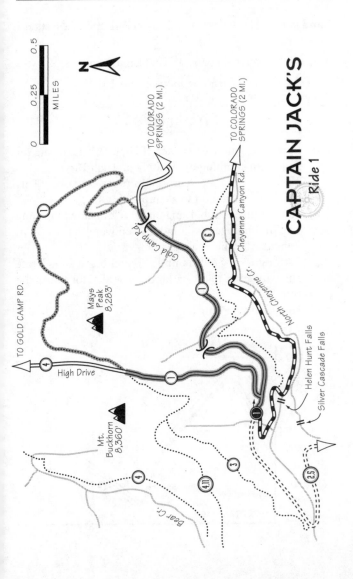

CAPTAIN JACK'S
Ride 1

TO COLORADO SPRINGS (2 MI.)

TO COLORADO SPRINGS (2 MI.)

Gold Camp Rd.

Cheyenne Canyon Rd.

North Cheyenne Cr.

Helen Hunt Falls

Silver Cascade Falls

High Drive

TO GOLD CAMP RD.

Mays Peak
8,283'

Mt. Buckhorn
8,360'

Bear Cr.

MILES
0   0.25   0.5

N

Land status: North Cheyenne Canyon Park and Pike National Forest.

Maps: Pike National Forest; USGS Manitou Springs.

Access: High Drive parking lot. See page 15.

The ride:

- 0.0   Leave the southeast corner of High Drive parking lot and begin climbing moderately on High Drive.
- 1.0   Turn right onto the Penrose Multi-use Trail 665. (This junction is common to a couple of trails.)
- 1.2   Top of initial climb. Hang on for a long downhill run.
- 3.1   The trail plunges even more steeply and rates a 3+ in difficulty for the final 0.4 mile.
- 3.5   Turn right on Gold Camp Road and begin a moderate climb to return to the parking lot. Be alert for cars in the tunnel.
- 5.4   High Drive parking lot.

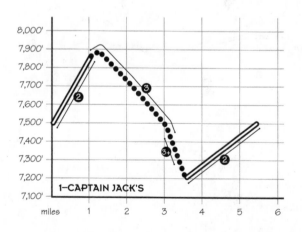

Gold Camp Road

Location: North Cheyenne Canyon Park, 5 miles west of Colorado Springs.

Distance: 29.2 miles up and back.

Time: Varies by distance. Figure about 4 hours up and back for the full distance.

Tread: 29.2 miles of dirt road in excellent shape. A short singletrack section detours around a collapsed tunnel.

Aerobic level: Easy; moderate, or strenuous. The rating of this gradual climb will depend on the distance ridden. Riding to Cripple Creek is much more strenuous than riding to the St. Mary's trailhead.

Technical difficulty: 2.

Highlights: A scenic and peaceful ride. Cars are forbidden on this road, creating a wide playground for bikes. Views of the plains and North Cheyenne Canyon unfold beneath as the road twists into the mountains. Cars are allowed at the 8.4-mile mark. Gold Camp Road links with Jones's Downhill (Ride 11), Mount Baldy (Ride 10), and St. Mary's (Ride 5).

Land status: Pike National Forest.

Maps: Pike National Forest; USGS Manitou Springs and Mount Big Chief.

Access: High Drive parking lot. See page 15.

The ride:

0.0   Leave the High Drive parking lot via the closed portion of Gold Camp Road marked by a large green gate on the northwest corner of the lot. The road climbs steadily at a moderate clip.

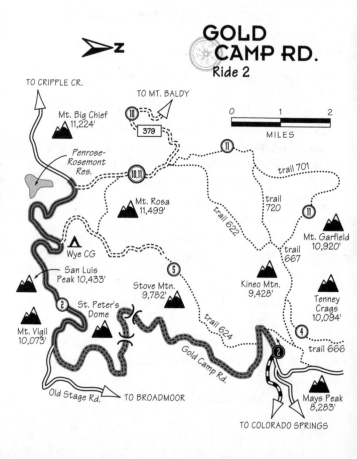

GOLD CAMP RD.

Ride 2

1.1 Turn left onto the St. Mary's Trail. This is a detour for the collapsed tunnel.

1.2 Take the left fork and return to the road. The St. Mary's Trail continues to the right (see Ride 5).

4.8 The first of two tunnels.

8.4 Turn right as Old Stage Road merges with Gold Camp Road. Cars are allowed from this point onward. Left returns to Colorado Springs near the Cheyenne Mountain Zoo.

8.8 Keep right on Gold Camp Road.

9.3 Stay left on Gold Camp Road.

12.4 Pass Wye Campground off to the right. The grade eases.

14.6 Junction with Mount Baldy Road (Forest Road 379) on right. Decision time! Turn around for a great downhill run back to the High Drive parking lot. Or turn right onto FR 379 for Jones' Downhill (see Ride 11) and the area's best singletrack downhill. Either way returns to the High Drive parking lot. True mileage junkies can stay left on Gold Camp Road and pedal another 20 miles to Colorado Highway 67 and the town of Cripple Creek (arrange a vehicle shuttle beforehand).

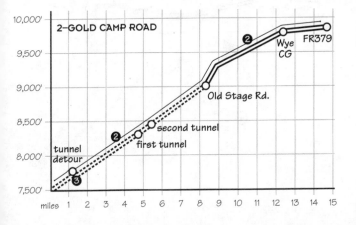

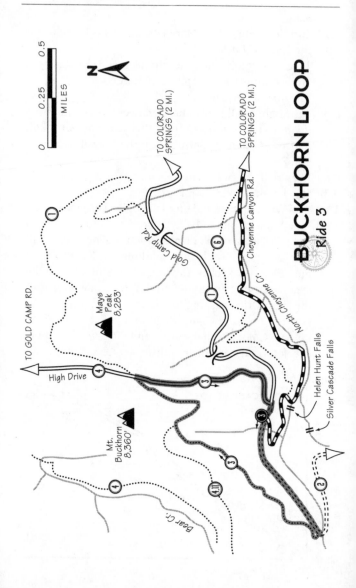

BUCKHORN LOOP
Ride 3

Buckhorn Loop
(Captain Jack's Frontside)

Location: North Cheyenne Canyon Park, 5 miles west of Colorado Springs.

Distance: 3.9-mile loop.

Time: 30 to 45 minutes.

Tread: 2.2 miles of singletrack and 1.7 miles of dirt road. The hard-packed, dirt singletrack is in good shape, but the last 0.5 mile is gravelly.

Aerobic level: Moderate. The singletrack is a fairly constant climb.

Technical difficulty: 3. Surf is in the form of roots, rocks, and gravel.

Highlights: Buckhorn is a great "quick fix" that lunch-hour commandos will want on their menus. Just enough uphill to pump the legs, plenty of down, and technical sections to keep the brain awake. Ride clockwise or be prepared to leap from the trail to avoid other cyclists.

Land status: Pike National Forest and North Cheyenne Canyon Park.

Maps: Pike National Forest, USGS Manitou Springs.

Access: High Drive lot. See page 15.

The ride:

0.0 Leave the High Drive parking lot via the closed portion of Gold Camp Road marked by a large green gate on the northwest corner of the lot. The road is closed to cars, not bikes.

0.6 Turn right on Buckhorn Trail directly before the sweeping, left-hand hairpin turn. (Watch for this discreet trail on the right side of the road, 30 yards after a small metal sign (*No vehicle use off this road*) and about the same distance before the sign for North Cheyenne Creek.)

0.7 After this first pitch there is a switchback and a trail to the left. Keep right and follow the switchback.

2.0 Turn right at the T junction onto the Jones Park Multi-use Trail 667. Left leads down to the Bear Creek Trail (see Ride 4) or beyond on a long ride to Lake Moraine.

2.8 Turn right on High Road and descend to the parking lot. This junction also connects to two other rides: either cross the road to Trail 665 (see Ride 1), or turn left and descend to the Palmer Trail (see Ride 8).

3.9 High Drive parking lot.

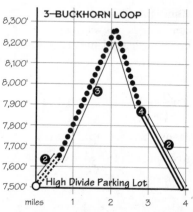

Bear Creek Loop

Location: 3 miles west of Colorado Springs and 2 miles south of Manitou Springs.

Distance: 8.3 miles

Time: 1.5 hours.

Tread: 3.5 miles of singletrack, 4.2 miles of dirt road, and 0.6 miles of paved road. Loose gravel is prevalent in Bear Canyon.

Aerobic level: Moderate. The ride starts with an 1,800-foot climb in under 4 miles.

Technical difficulty: 3+. The surf gets a bit rough in Bear Canyon.

Highlights: The downhill section is scenic and exhilarating. In Bear Canyon loose gravel and occasional rocks paired with distracting views can endo the best riders. Stop as needed to admire the view and then hang on to enjoy the thrill ride down. Watch for car traffic on High Drive.

Land status: Bear Creek Canyon Park and Pike National Forest.

Maps: Pike National Forest; USGS Manitou Springs.

Access: Park in the Section 16 lot. From Colorado Springs, drive west on CO 24 and turn left onto 21st Street. Then turn right onto Lower Gold Camp Road. Continue straight at the four-way stop. The Section 16 parking lot is on the right with additional parking just down the road. In summer, parking is allowed on High Drive (see page 15).

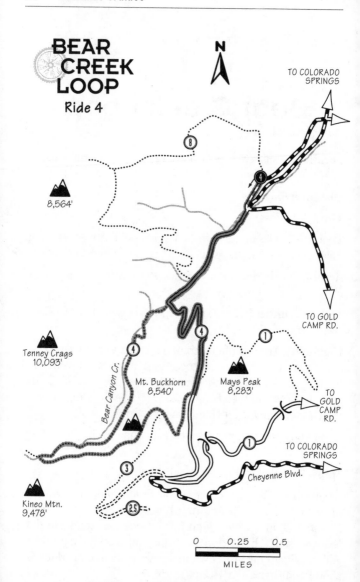

BEAR CREEK LOOP
Ride 4

N

TO COLORADO SPRINGS

8

8,564'

4

TO GOLD CAMP RD.

Tenney Crags
10,093'

4

Mt. Buckhorn
8,540'

4

Mays Peak
8,283'

1

TO GOLD CAMP RD.

Bear Canyon Cr.

1

TO COLORADO SPRINGS

3

Cheyenne Blvd.

Kineo Mtn.
9,478'

2.5

0   0.25   0.5

MILES

The ride:

0.0   From the Section 16 parking lot head west up Gold Camp Road.

0.3   Turn right at the all-way stop sign and cross the gate for High Drive. If it's closed for the season, use the small step on the side. Continue the moderate climb up High Drive.

1.0   The Palmer Trail (see Ride 8) goes right; stay on the road.

1.4   The Lower Bear Creek Trail goes right; stay on road curving left.

2.8   Turn right at the top of High Drive onto the Jones Park Trail 667. This is a busy section of trail with two-way traffic, including riders on Captain Jack's (see Ride 1).

3.6   The trail forks; keep right on the Jones Park Trail. The Buckhorn Trail (see Ride 3) goes left.

4.8   Turn right onto Trail 666 and hold on for the wild ride down Bear Canyon.

6.9   Retrace the route to the parking lot by turning left on High Drive.

8.3   Section 16 parking lot.

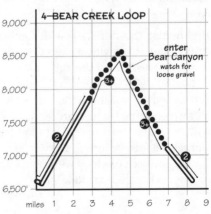

St. Mary's Falls

Location: North Cheyenne Canyon, 5 miles west of Colorado Springs.

Distance: 7.3 miles one-way to Mount Baldy Road; or do a 16.8-mile loop by taking Jones' Downhill (see Ride 11).

Time: 3 hours out and back. The loop takes 4 hours.

Tread: 4.9 miles of singletrack and 2.4 miles of dirt road. Erosion has rutted the beginning of the dirt road and a downed tree crosses the upper singletrack.

Aerobic level: Strenuous. This ride in its entirety is not for the timid. Its rating stems more from the length of the entire ascent rather than steepness. But it is very steep by the falls.

Technical difficulty: 3+. Tight switchbacks and eroding steeps create some sections of class 4 riding.

Highlights: This ride starts with a mild ascent through pine, spruce, and aspen with Buffalo Creek in sight. In fact, many people ride just this stretch and return. Grunt out the steeps by St. Mary's Falls to ride through the tailings of an old mine. From here the ride is moderate. The trail to Mount Baldy Road offers narrow singletrack and more glimpses of Colorado's mining past. St. Mary's does have a lot of unmarked side trails. No worries if a turn is missed, though, just more work. This is a fun out and back or a loop with Gold Camp Road (see Ride 2), or Jones's Downhill (see Ride 11).

ST. MARY'S FALLS
Ride 5

N

Mays Peak 8,283'

High Drive
Gold Camp Rd.

trail 667

Kineo Mtn. 9,478'

trail 720

trail 668

St. Mary's Falls

trail 701

Stove Mtn. 9,782'

Mt. Baldy 12,226'

379

624

Mt. Rosa 11,499'

Mt. Big Chief 11,224'

TO ELK PARK

TO CRIPPLE CREEK (17 MI.)

Old Stage Rd.

TO COLORADO SPRINGS

Cheyenne Blvd.

0   0.5   1
MILES

Land status: Pike National Forest. A short section near Mount Baldy Road skirts private land.

Maps: Pike National Forest; USGS Manitou Springs, Big Chief.

Access: High Drive parking lot (see page 15 for directions).

The ride:

0.0 Leave the High Drive parking lot via the closed portion of Gold Camp Road marked by a large green gate on the northwest corner of the lot. The road is closed to cars but not bikes.

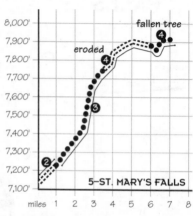

1.1 The tunnel here has collapsed. The main route now detours onto the St. Mary's Trail. Leave the road on the left and climb above the tunnel.

1.2 At the fork, turn right. A sign for the falls (1.75 miles ahead) marks the way.

2.4 Junction; keep right. A metal sign gives the distance to the falls as 0.2 mile.

2.6 Again, keep right at the sign. Left goes to the falls.

3.2 Keep right. Left heads to the creek.

3.5 Keep right as the trail becomes an old doubletrack.

3.9 Right at the fork to a steep, rocky incline.

4.0 Keep left as a road joins from the right.

4.6 An old mine lies on this eroded hill with lots of intersecting roads. The proper road is labeled 624. Keep on this main road and enjoy some downhill.

6.2 Go straight across the intersection marked on the left with a small cement structure. In about 10 meters leave Road 624 for the trail on the right. A marker for Road

624 stands beside the trail but points to the road.

6.4   Turn right after a short, steep downhill where a singletrack leaves the road. The area is recognizable by three dead stumps. Take the singletrack and immediately cross a trickling stream.

6.6   A fallen tree impedes the way. Heavy surf, dude!

7.3   Junction with Mount Baldy Road (FR 379). To create a loop, turn right onto Mount Baldy Road and pedal 1 mile onto Jones' Downhill (see Ride 11). Left continues on to Gold Camp Road (see Ride 2).

Columbine

Location: North Cheyenne Canyon, 3 miles west of Colorado Springs.

Distance: 3.8 miles one way.

Time: 1 hour.

Tread: Wide singletrack the whole way. Surf is up with sections of loose gravel.

Aerobic level: Moderate due to loose gravel climbs.

Technical difficulty: 3. The switchbacks paired with loose gravel are tricky.

Highlights: The Columbine trail offers spectacular vistas of the canyon and the Broadmoor below. The rock walls and ledges are divine during wildflower season. Look for columbine,

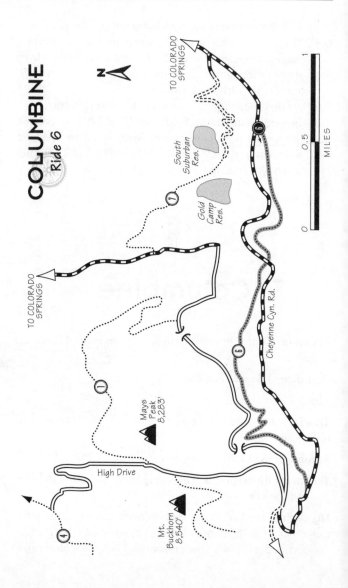

Colorado's state flower. There was talk of closing this crowded trail to bikes. Yet, at press time, it was still open. Columbine loops well with The Chutes (see Ride 7).

Land status: North Cheyenne Canyon Park.

Maps: USGS Manitou Springs.

Access: Take Cheyenne Boulevard westbound to North Cheyenne Park. Keep right on Cheyenne at the entrance to Seven Falls. Park at the trailhead, less than 0.1 mile up the road on the left. There is also a parking lot at the Discovery Center.

The ride:

0.0 The singletrack, marked with a small sign, leaves from the left side of the small parking area. Immediately cross the creek and climb a short hill to a picnic area. The singletrack here is 5 feet wide, hard packed, and level.

0.25 Continue straight through two more picnic areas. The old stonework in the stream is a gaging station.

0.5 Turn left at the trail marker as you leave this last picnic area. The trail switchbacks and becomes level, skirting a narrow ledge and rock wall.

0.8 Cross a wide bridge and STOP before crossing the busy road. The trail is easily picked up on

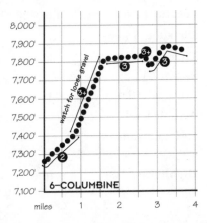

the other side.

1.0   The middle trailhead.

1.1   Loose gravel marks the start of some 3+ switchbacks that quickly gain elevation.

1.4   An old trail leading away to the left is closed; bear right. The gradient eases.

2.8   Keep right after going down some tight switchbacks and through some large rocks. The small trail on the left is closed. The main trail then climbs again.

3.8   Upper trailhead. To connect to other trails turn right and climb 0.5 mile. Grab a look at the map and pick a trail. A good loop back to the car is The Chutes (Ride 7).

The Chutes

Location: 2 miles west of Colorado Springs.

Distance: 3.1 miles one way.

Time: 45 minutes up; 15 minutes down.

Tread: 1.1 miles of hard-packed singletrack, 1.1 miles of dirt road, and 0.9 mile of paved road.

Aerobic level: Moderate. This ride is short but fairly steep.

Technical difficulty: 3. The bermed corners on the way down add a bit to the difficulty and the fun.

Highlights: This ride's bermed turns give the downhill a bobsled feel. Too bad it's so short. Watch for people making the

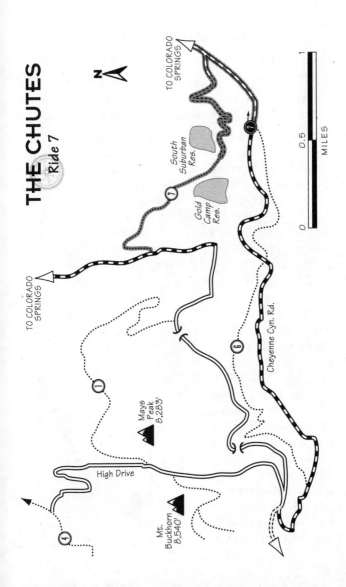

THE CHUTES
Ride 7

N

TO COLORADO SPRINGS

TO COLORADO SPRINGS

South Suburban Res.

Gold Camp Res.

①

①

⑦

⑥

④

Mays Peak 8,283'

Mt. Buckhorn 8,540'

High Drive

Cheyenne Cyn. Rd.

0   0.5   1

MILES

climb while going downhill! Combine this with the Columbine Trail (see Ride 6) for a great loop.

Land status: North Cheyenne Mountain Park and private holdings.

Maps: USGS Colorado Springs. The junction of The Chutes and Gold Camp Road is on the Manitou Springs quad.

Access: Take Cheyenne Boulevard westbound to North Cheyenne Canyon Park. Turn right and park in one of the designated pull-outs on Cheyenne Boulevard. There is also a parking lot at the Discovery Center. The ride description starts at the Discovery Center. To find The Chutes Trail from the High Drive Parking lot, follow Gold Camp Road downhill. The trailhead is on the right, 0.4 mile from the pavement's start, at a parking area. A park regulations sign marks the area. The trail leaves from the left side of the parking lot in the same direction as the road.

The ride:

0.0   Ride toward town on Cheyenne Boulevard.
0.7   Turn left onto Ridgeway.
0.9   Turn right at the horse pasture (a small clearing with lots of no parking signs). The route follows the dirt road.
1.0   Go around the gate and start up the dirt road. All singletrack in this immediate area is closed to bikes.

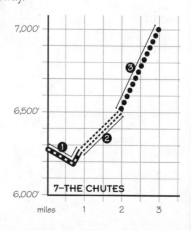

1.8   The road forks. Either way leads to the same place. Go left to keep even with the odometer readings given here.

2.0   Both roads arrive at Gold Camp Reservoir.

2.1   Roads join; bank onto the singletrack and begin a more earnest climb.

2.9   The trail switchbacks left. Stay on the main track, ignoring the minor trail to the right.

3.1   Gold Camp Road. Retrace your tracks to Cheyenne Boulevard, or turn left on Gold Camp Road to make a loop with the Columbine Trail (Ride 6).

Palmer Trail–
Section 16 Loop

Location: 3 miles west of the Colorado Springs and 2 miles south of Manitou Springs.

Distance: 5.8-mile loop.

Time: 1.5 hours.

Tread: 4.8 miles of singletrack, 0.8 mile of dirt road, and 0.2 mile of paved road. Expect good conditions with the exception of Section 16, which resembles a steep, empty streambed.

Aerobic level: Moderate.

Technical difficulty: 3. The upper portion of the Section 16 downhill rates a 5+.

PALMER TRAIL— SECTION 16 LOOP

Ride 8

Intemann Trail

Section 16 trail

Bear Creek Rd.

8,130'

8,564'

Hunter's Run

Palmer Trail

Gold Camp Rd.

Old Scout Camp

High Drive

N

0   0.25   0.5
MILES

Highlights: Old pine forests, tumbling streams, and ruins keep the mind off the gradual climb. The view from the top of the Crystal Park spur is spectacular, but stop before the Crystal Park subdivision. Many riders stick to the Palmer Trail for an up-and-back ride because erosion has made the Section 16 descent treacherous. It's basically a steep wash that challenges even the best riders.

Land status: Bear Creek Canyon Park and Pike National Forest.

Maps: Pike National Forest; USGS Manitou Springs.

Access: From Colorado Springs drive west on U.S. Highway 24 and turn left onto 21st Street. Then turn right onto Lower Gold Camp Road. Continue straight at the four-way stop. The Section 16 parking lot is on the right with additional parking just down the road. In summer parking is allowed on High Drive.

The ride:

- 0.0   From the Section 16 trailhead parking lot, head west up Gold Camp Road.
- 0.3   Turn right at the all-way stop sign and cross the gate for High Drive. If it's closed for the season, use the steps on the side.
- 0.9   A trail comes off the road at a 30-degree angle. This is an alternate trailhead. The official one is just ahead.
- 1.0   Turn right at the small, rusty metal gate marking the trailhead proper. The alternate trail joins in 0.1 mile ahead.

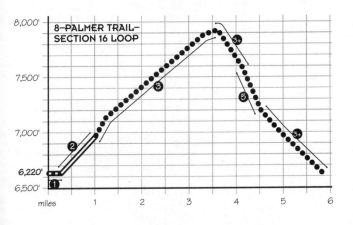

1.2   Turn right, doubling back on a switchback. Another trail continues ahead to an old scout camp. All that remains is a chimney and the foundation to the wash house.

3.3   Decision time. The loop—and this description—turns right to Section 16. It gets very technical. The left fork ascends toward Crystal Park and a wonderful view of the Garden of the Gods. Going left, it's 0.3 mile to the overlook and the end of the trail at a private property line. Any farther is trespassing.

4.0   Turn left at this small fork and head down. The right simply peters out at a small overlook.

4.1   The trail descends a wash. Loose gravel and rocks abound. A technical rating of 5+!

4.5   This small clearing can be confusing. Follow the trail to the right and down.

4.9   Pass by the Paul Intemann Memorial Trail (see Ride 9). The tread gets easier from here. But keep awake for rock drop-offs and people.

5.8   Back at the parking lot.

Paul Intemann Memorial Trail

Location: 3 miles west of Colorado Springs and 2 miles south of Manitou Springs.

Distance: 5 miles out and back.

Time: 1 hour.

Tread: 5 miles of singletrack.

Aerobic level: Mostly easy. Only a few brief climbs.

Technical difficulty: 4. Tight, rocky switchbacks on this one!

Highlights: An excellent technical test! Many different obstacles make a clean ride tough. Unfortunately the trail isn't complete. It's scheduled to connect to Manitou Springs. For now, it ends shortly after crossing the Crystal Park road. There are some log steps along the route that force many riders to dismount. I had a flat tire along this trail; watch for sharp rocks and cactus.

Land status: A variety of private holdings surround this one. A sign marks the end of the ride.

Maps: USGS Manitou Springs.

Access: From Colorado Springs drive west on U.S. Highway 24 and turn left onto 21st Street. Turn right on Lower Gold Camp Road. Continue straight at the four-way stop. The Section 16 parking lot is on the right with additional parking just down the road.

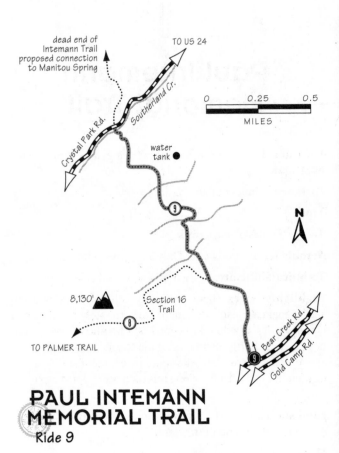

dead end of
Intemann Trail
proposed connection
to Manitou Spring

TO US 24

Southerland Cr.

Crystal Park Rd.

water
tank ●

0   0.25   0.5

MILES

9

N

8,130'

Section 16
Trail

8

TO PALMER TRAIL

Bear Creek Rd.

9

Gold Camp Rd.

PAUL INTEMANN
MEMORIAL TRAIL
Ride 9

The ride:

0.0   Begin climbing on the Section 16 trail from the parking
      lot.
0.7   The well-marked Intemann Trail leads off to the right,
      climbing for another 0.2 mile and then twisting down-
      hill for more than a mile.
2.2   Crystal Park Road. The trail picks up again just down
      the road to the right. Again, it is well marked. Many
      riders will want to turn around here to avoid the steps
      ahead.
2.5   One last sign marks the end of the trail.

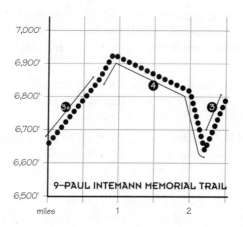

Mount Baldy

Location: 15 miles west of Colorado Springs.

Distance: 12.2 miles out and back.

Time: 2.5 hours.

Tread: 12.2 miles of four-wheel-drive road with patches of sand and loose gravel.

Aerobic level: Strenuous. The trail climbs constantly from its beginning elevation of 9,800 feet to its end at 11,840 feet. The return descent has a tendency to leave arms and legs aching for home.

Technical difficulty: 2+. This is a pretty straightforward trail. Its main difficulties come from the sandy patches. Momentum and weight distribution are the key.

Highlights: The view from the top is one of the best in the neighborhood. Kansas is visible to the east, Pike's Peak looms in the north, and the short alpine wildflower season delivers a rare treat. The downhill is fun, but soft spots and a few water bars can make things a bit hairy. A gate at the top of the ride marks land managed by the Colorado Springs Water Department.

Land status: Pike National Forest and Colorado Springs Water Department, (719) 636-5616. Bikers must stop at the gate short of the summit. In the future, the city water department may allow bikers.

Maps: Pike National Forest; USGS Manitou Springs.

MOUNT BALDY
Ride 10

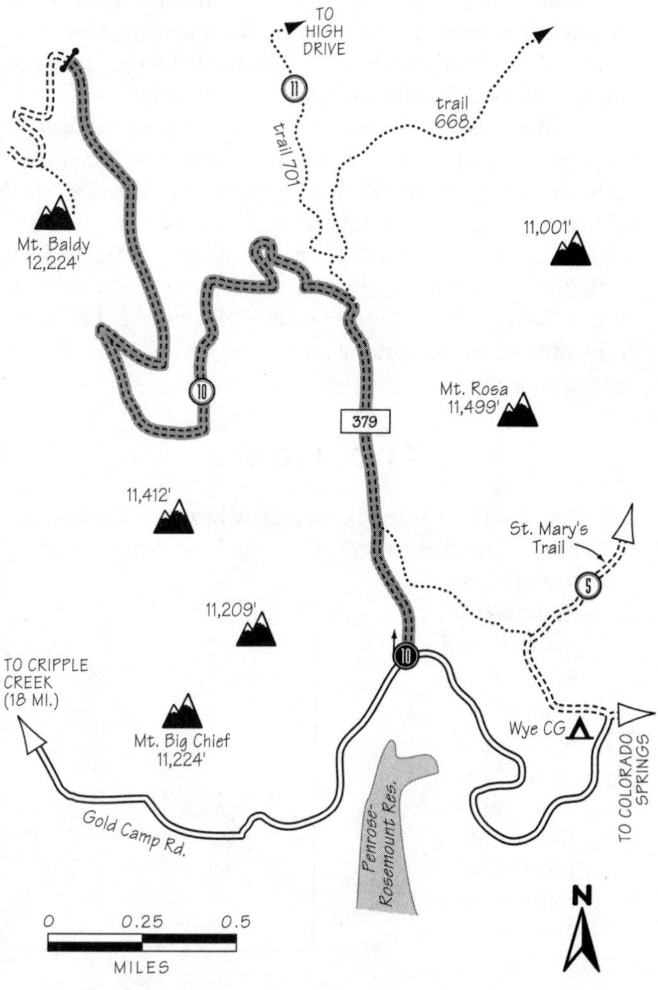

TO
HIGH
DRIVE

11

trail 701

trail 668

11,001'

Mt. Baldy
12,224'

10

Mt. Rosa
11,499'

379

11,412'

St. Mary's
Trail

5

11,209'

TO CRIPPLE
CREEK
(18 MI.)

10

Mt. Big Chief
11,224'

Wye CG

TO COLORADO SPRINGS

Gold Camp Rd.

Penrose-
Rosemount Res.

0   0.25   0.5

MILES

N

Access: This ride is accessed off of the Old Stage Coach Road out of the Broadmoor. From Colorado Springs drive south on Colorado Highway 115 to CO 122 and turn right. This road becomes Lake Avenue. Keep right on Lake Avenue and circumnavigate the Broadmoor. Turn left on El Pomar Park Road and follow the signs toward the zoo. This road changes names a couple of times but is easily followed. Look for Old Stage Coach Road to fork away to the right as the left fork goes to the zoo. This junction is at Cheyenne Mountain and Penrose boulevards. The road winds and turns to dirt in about 1 mile. Stay right at the first fork. Again, keep right where the road to Emerald Ranch enters in (4 miles from the end of pavement). Stay on the main road. Pass the Wye Campground and park at Mount Baldy Road (Forest Road 379) in the Penrose-Rosemount Reservoir parking area on the left, 12.2 miles from pavement's end.

The ride:

0.0 Start up FR 379 and immediately begin to climb to the north. The climb is consistent and the surface good. A few roads and trails join the main road. Stay on the main road.

1.7 Stay on the main road. The trail on the right is Jones's Downhill (see Ride 11).

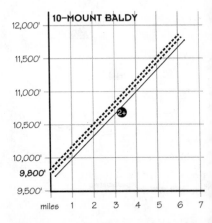

4.3 Take the right fork. The left fork heads over to Elk Park.

6.1 End of the line. The road continues ahead, but for now it's closed to bikes. Check with the Colorado Springs Water Department for current status.

Jones's Downhill

Location: 15 miles southwest of the Broadmoor.

Distance: 10.2 miles one way. This ride, as described, involves shuttling vehicles.

Time: 2 hours plus sightseeing time.

Tread: 8.5 miles of singletrack and 1.7 miles of four-wheel-drive road. New construction in the Jones Park region has softened the tread.

Aerobic level: Moderate. Yup, it's nearly all downhill and still ranks as moderate.

Technical difficulty: 3+. Water bars, rocky patches, and new construction all combine with speed for this rating.

Highlights: Downhill, downhill, and more downhill! Whoop-te-doos in the middle of aspen groves and Jones Park make for the ultimate downhill run in the area. The Forest Service is in the midst of some trail construction here. Not to worry, though. When confused, simply point the tires down the fall line. All the side trails will funnel back to Trail 667 or 668. As described here, this ride ends at the High Drive parking lot. But many other options exist. Bring the map and invent a new combination. This trail makes an excellent downhill leg for Gold Camp Road or St. Mary's Trail (see rides 2 and 5).

Land status: Pike National Forest.

Maps: Pike National Forest; USGS Manitou Springs.

Access: This ride is accessed off of the Old Stage Coach Road out of the Broadmoor. From Colorado Springs drive south on Colorado 115 and turn right onto CO 122. This road becomes Lake Avenue. Keep right on Lake Avenue and circumnavigate the Broadmoor. Turn left on El Pomar Park Road and follow the signs toward the zoo. This road changes names a couple of times but is easily followed. Look for Old Stage Coach Road to fork to the right as the left fork goes to the zoo. This junction is at Cheyenne Mountain and Penrose boulevards. The road winds and turns to dirt in about 1 mile (set your odometer to 0 miles here). Stay right at the first fork (in 2.5 miles). Again, keep right where the road to Emerald Ranch enters (at 4 miles). Stay on the main road, pass the Wye Campground, and park at Mount Baldy Road (Forest Road 379) in the Penrose-Rosemount Reservoir parking area on the left (12.2 miles from pavement's end). If the shuttle vehicle has four-wheel-drive, continue up FR 379 to Trail 701.

The ride:

- **0.0** Head up FR 379 and stay on it. St. Mary's Trail (Ride 5) joins in from across the creek at 0.7 mile.
- **1.7** Turn right onto Trail 701 and begin the roller coaster downhill. (FR 379 continues to the top of Mount Baldy; see Ride 10.)
- **1.8** Trail 668 zips past on the right; stay straight on Trail 701.

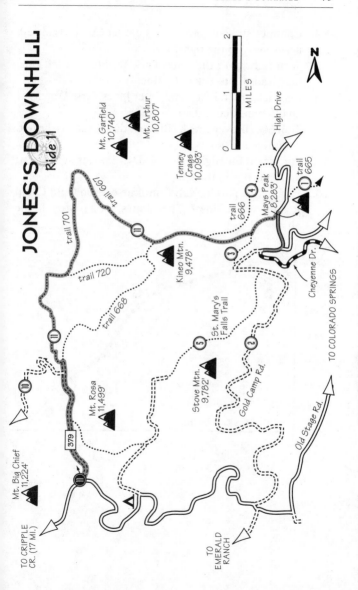

4.4   Continue straight ahead. The Forester Cutoff, Trail 720, heads away to the right.

5.5   Turn right onto the Jones Park Trail 667. A left turn here leads up to Lake Moraine.

6.4   Keep left on Trail 667 and enter Jones Park. Watch for an old mine about 0.4 mile ahead.

7.3   Trail 666, Beaver Creek (Ride 4), disappears to the left. Continue on Trail 667.

9.2   Turn right on High Drive. Ride 1 goes straight ahead and Ride 8 is to the left.

10.2 High Drive parking lot. Continue east on Gold Camp Road to reach Ride 7, The Chutes, for a route into the city.

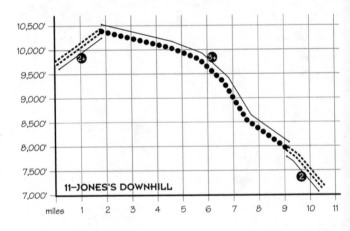

Barr Trail

Location: Manitou Springs.

Distance: 11.7 miles one way.

Time: At least 4 hours to go up. The downhill takes about 2 hours depending on traffic.

Tread: 11.7 miles of singletrack.

Aerobic level: Strenuous. Strenuous is an understatement if ridden from the bottom. Riding down is aerobically easy.

Technical difficulty: 4-. The main obstacle is the climb. However, those who brave the upper portion will find obstacles and tight switchbacks.

Highlights: While most folks will want to turn around at Barr Camp, it's theoretically possible to ride to the summit. The toll road goes to the summit for those who find a willing friend to drive a shuttle vehicle. However you ride it, Barr Trail is one tough cookie with more than 7,000 feet in altitude change! Try to enjoy the spectacular views while struggling to take in the ever-decreasing oxygen. Watch out for other travelers on this busy trail!

Land status: Pike National Forest.

Maps: Pike National Forest; USGS Manitou Springs, Pike's Peak.

Access: From Manitou Springs follow the signs to the Cog Railway. Take Ruxton Avenue south from downtown and follow it

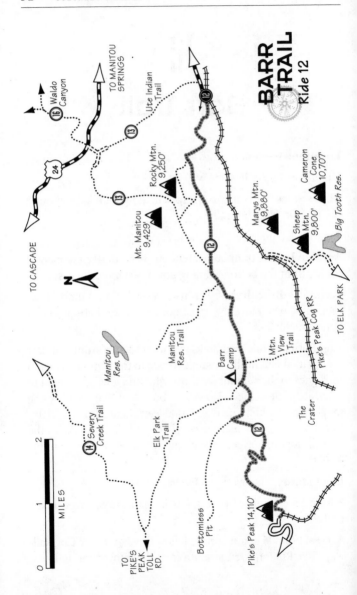

past the railway's depot. Turn right into the trailhead parking lot. The trail begins on the south side of the lot.

The ride:

0.0 Start up the switchbacks. These first 3 miles are the toughest.

2.4 The Incline Trail's lower trailhead passes by on the right.

2.6 The experimental forest and upper Incline Trail pass by on the right. Ride 13 departs from here.

3.2 Stay on the main trail as the Manitou Reservoir trail disappears to the right

4.4 The Mountain View turnoff passes on the left and heads to the Cog Railroad. The most level portion of the ride starts here.

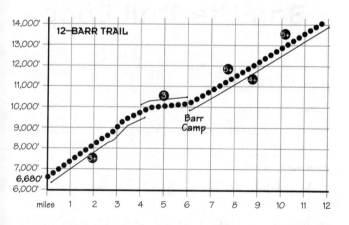

6.0 Barr Camp. Most people turn around here. Heck, camp out in a cabin! The Elk Park Trail heads west from here. Those going to the summit continue south on the Barr Trail.

7.0 Keep left. The right fork heads to an area called The Bottomless Pit.

8.7 There is a shelter here that should have water. Climb 2,110 feet in 3 miles and hit the summit!

11.7 Welcome to the summit of Pike's Peak and the view that inspired the words to *America the Beautiful*.

Barr-Ute Trail Loop

Location: Manitou Springs.

Distance: 8.8-mile loop.

Time: 1.5 to 2 hours.

Tread: 5.3 miles of singletrack, 3 miles of dirt road, and 0.5 mile of paved road.

Aerobic level: Strenuous.

Technical difficulty: 4-. Watch for heavily eroded sections on the downhill portion.

Highlights: The downhill on Long Ranch Road arguably makes the climb worthwhile. While the downhill is fast and furious, the climb gains more than 2,000 feet in 3 miles! The views are up close and personal with Pike's Peak. The lower section fol-

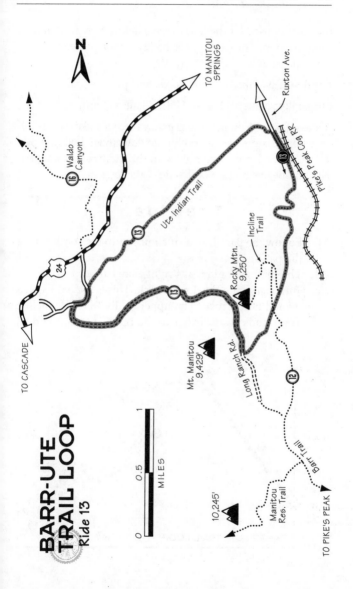

BARR-UTE
TRAIL LOOP
Ride 13

MILES
0   0.5   1

TO CASCADE

24

13

13

13

16
Waldo
Canyon

Ute Indian Trail

Mt. Manitou
9,429'

Rocky Mtn.
9,250'

Incline
Trail

Long Ranch Rd.

10,245'

Manitou
Res. Trail

Barr Trail

12

TO PIKE'S PEAK

TO MANITOU
SPRINGS

Ruxton Ave.

Pike's Peak Cog RR

13

N

lows a trail used by the Ute Indians before they were forced from the land. This section has had some tough times of late. Obey all signs!

Land status: Pike National Forest and private holdings.

Maps: Pike National Forest; USGS Manitou Springs, Cascade.

Access: From Manitou Springs follow the signs to the Cog Railway. Take Ruxton Avenue south from downtown. Follow it past the railway's depot. Turn right into the trailhead parking lot. The trail begins on the south side of the lot.

The ride:

0.0 Follow the Barr Trail as it climbs from the south side of the parking lot.

2.4 The Incline Trail breaks right; stay left.

2.6 Turn right onto the doubletrack. This is the old Experimental Forest road. The upper trailhead of the Incline Trail heads away farther to the right. Just up the road

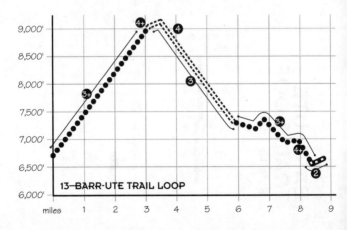

are some old foundations the Forest Service used when monitoring the non-native trees planted in the Experimental Forest.

3.0   Keep right and climb or push up the eroded road.
3.1   Turn right onto Long Ranch Road.
3.5   Start the downhill!
5.8   Turn right on the dirt road. Then take the next right less than 0.1 mile down hill.
6.6   The power lines now follow the road.
7.9   Pass by the filtration plant and head down into Manitou Springs.
8.3   Turn right onto Ruxton Avenue and return to the trailhead.
8.8   Trailhead.

Elk Park-Severy Downhill

Location: Near the town of Cascade, 10 miles west of Colorado Springs.

Distance: 6.3 miles one way.

Time: 1 hour for a downhill run or 3 hours up and back.

Tread: 6.3 miles of singletrack. The uppermost portions look like a dirt road but ride like singletrack. The middle of the ride is extremely rocky.

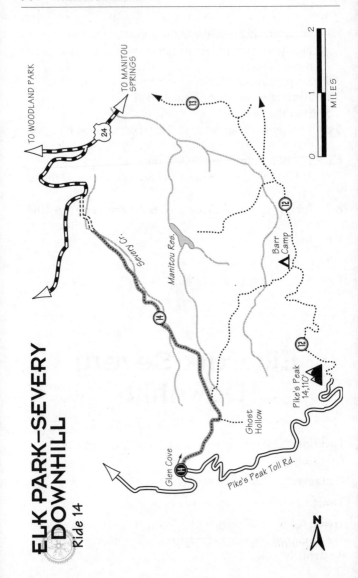

ELK PARK–SEVERY DOWNHILL
Ride 14

TO WOODLAND PARK

TO MANITOU SPRINGS

24

13

12

Severy Cr.

Manitou Res.

Barr Camp

14

12

Ghost Hollow

Pike's Peak 14,110'

Glen Cove

14

Pike's Peak Toll Rd.

N

MILES

0   1   2

Aerobic level: Moderate. Strenuous when ridden uphill.

Technical difficulty: 4-. Some sections of the upper Severy Trail are 5+.

Highlights: This is a truly unspoiled stretch of woods. Unfortunately some of those woods lie fallen across the trail. The middle section is extremely steep and is marked only with cairns. The lower trail parallels Severy Creek as it cascades down boulders amongst pine and aspen. I have described this as a shuttle-ride from the top. Without a shuttle, ride it from the bottom. The trail can be accessed only off of the Pike's Peak Toll Road. But if you ride from the bottom a discount on the toll is given. Be sure to check the road's closing time; don't get stuck inside when the gates close!

Land status: Pike National Forest.

Maps: Pike National Forest; USGS Cascade, Woodland Park, and Pikes Peak.

Access: From Colorado Springs drive 11 miles west on U.S. Highway 24 to Cascade. Turn left into Cascade, then right, and follow the signs to the Pike's Peak Toll Road. Pay appropriate toll and head up the road. The lower trailhead is accessed by a dirt road on the left, 1.5 miles from the gate. It dips down just before a large boulder. Drive 0.5 mile and park on the right. The trail starts just ahead at the trail bridge. The upper trailhead is 1 mile past Glen Cove. The trail follows an old road steeply off to the left. It is just before the metal winter-closure gate.

The ride:

0.0   Dip steeply away from the toll road.

1.2   Ghost Hollow Junction; turn left. Ghost Hollow is an old mining camp 0.7 mile up the right-hand trail. The Cincinnati Mine struck water instead of gold and its motherlode still flows from the mine.

1.7 Turn left onto the Severy Creek Trail. The Elk Park Trail continues on the right to Barr Camp (see Ride 12).

2.5 The tread becomes more technical. A portage may be necessary.

2.9 The trail descends to Severy Creek and is less steep. Watch for downed trees.

6.3 The lower trailhead.

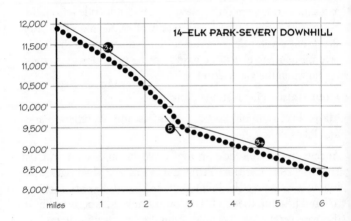

Falcon Trail

Location: United States Air Force Academy.

Distance: 10.9-mile loop.

Time: 2 hours.

Tread: 10.9 miles of singletrack and doubletrack.

Aerobic level: Moderate. While fairly level, the few steeps and obstacles justify the rating.

Technical difficulty: 4. Some riders may have to carry their bikes in a couple of spots.

Highlights: Take a look at what your tax dollars can make! The United States Air Force Academy is a beautiful installation and the Falcon Trail shows it off. It is well signed, with little white falcons, and offers diverse terrain. Odds are pretty good you'll see some of the local mule deer population. The map from the Visitor Center lists the sites, including the fascinating, old, pioneer home. Don't wander off the trail. Remember, this is a military base!

Land status: United States Air Force Academy.

Maps: USAFA map (available in the Visitor Center); USGS Cascade, Palmer Lake.

Access: Enter the Academy via the south gate, about 9 miles north of Colorado Springs on Interstate 25. After about 2 miles, turn left onto Pine Drive. Go another 3.5 miles and turn right onto Community Drive. After 1 more mile, turn right. Parking

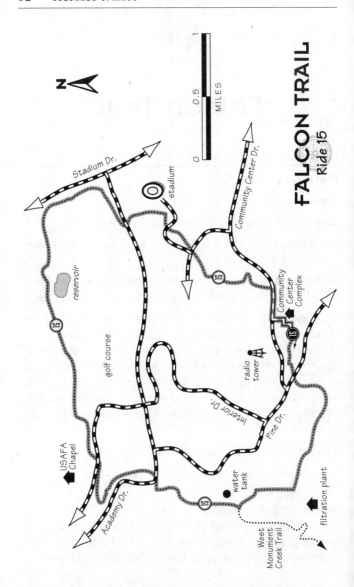

FALCON TRAIL
Ride 15

is available around the Community Center. The trail starts in the rear right corner (southwest) of the complex and is marked with a big blue sign.

The ride:

0.0 The trail is immediately technical. A portage here is nothing to be ashamed of.

0.5 Cross Pine Drive and then the creek. Keep following the sign of the falcon.

2.4 Keep right as the West Monument Creek Trail passes by.

3.5 Look before crossing Academy Drive!

4.7 Cross over Interior Drive.

5.2 Another road crossing. This one is Cross Drive. Gear down for an upcoming steep section.

6.3 Pass the reservoir.

8.1 Academy Drive. The USAFA football stadium is just ahead.

10.0 The trail enters the Community Center complex. Do you remember where you parked?

10.8 The loop is completed.

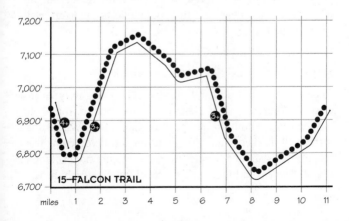

15–FALCON TRAIL

Waldo Canyon

Location: 2 miles west of Manitou Springs on US 24.

Distance: 7.5-mile loop.

Time: 1.5 to 2 hours depending on traffic.

Tread: 7.5 miles of hard-packed singletrack with some granite gravel sprinkled on top.

Aerobic level: Moderate.

Technical difficulty: 3+. Tight switchbacks, stretches of root-strewn tread, and granite wheel-grabbers add spice to Waldo.

Highlights: Views of Pike's Peak and Waldo Canyon and pedaling through an established forest with lichen-draped trees and moss-covered rocks make nice distractions. But Waldo is a popular guy and other traffic WILL be on the trail. Some unofficial side trails exist, but this route follows the main, well-worn singletrack.

Land status: Pike National Forest.

Maps: Pike National Forest; USGS Cascade.

Access: The trailhead is by the side of U.S. Highway 24 just west of Manitou Springs. Take US 24 westbound from Colorado Springs. About 3 miles past the Cave of the Winds Road is the well-marked Waldo Trail parking lot. If you come from Manitou, it is about 1.5 miles from the westbound on-ramp of US 24. Carry your bike up a long set of stairs to reach the trail.

WALDO CANYON
Ride 16

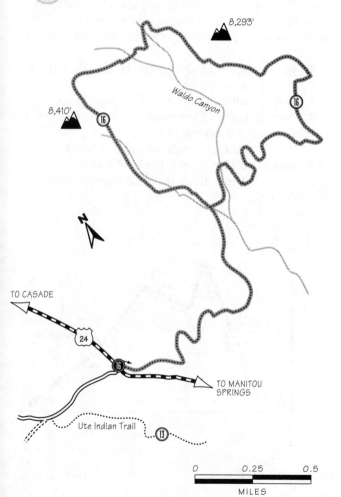

8,293'

Waldo Canyon

8,410'

16

16

N

TO CASADE

24

16

TO MANITOU
SPRINGS

Ute Indian Trail   13

0   0.25   0.5

MILES

The ride:

0.0   The trail proper starts up the stairs at the registration box. The odometer readings start from here.

0.3   Stay left. A trail goes right about 30 feet to some Pike's Peak granite.

0.9   Stay on the main trail. The small trail to the right overlooks Fountain Creek.

1.7   Take the left fork and climb hard along the stream.

2.5   Turn right at this T intersection. Just a bit farther to the downhill and switchbacks.

5.5   Hang on for a set of tight, twisty switchbacks.

5.8   Back at the fork. Keep left to head home.

7.5   Stick a fork in it. It's done! Please carry your bike down the steps.

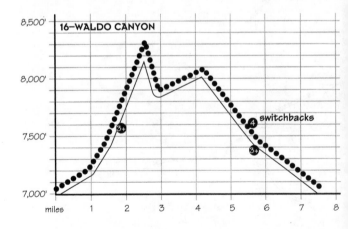

Woodland Park – Divide

Woodland Park lies 20 miles west of Colorado Springs on U.S. Highway 24, which continues on into Divide.

Woodland Park offers a full range of services with prices comparable to The Springs. Camping is also abundant in the surrounding hills. Rampart Reservoir offers three campgrounds and is the setting for Ride 17.

Woodland Park also has a couple of bike shops. If you forgot to bring along an extra tube, or want to look for a sale on shocks, roll up to the local shop.

The other focal point for visitors to this region is Divide, a small town 7 miles west of Woodland Park. Divide offers very limited services; gas and snacks are available. It is the closest civilization to Mueller State Park.

Mueller State Park has camping available for tents and recreational vehicles. These spots fill up quickly. Call ahead for reservations at (719) 687-2366. Three of this guide's rides are in this park.

Rampart Reservoir

Location: 10 miles southwest of Woodland Park.

Distance: 14-mile loop.

Time: 2 to 3 hours.

Tread: Excellent conditions throughout the 9.2 miles of singletrack, 3.1 miles of doubletrack, and 1.7 miles of paved road.

Aerobic level: Easy. Some brief climbs, but it's mostly level and long.

Technical difficulty: 2+. Smooth singletrack but sections of 5 can be sought out.

Highlights: This is *the* trail to introduce someone to mountain biking. The singletrack dodges around the reservoir among boulders and bushes, and numerous side trails offer endless variety for exploring. While suitable for beginners, gonzo riders won't have to look long for a challenge. Why doesn't everyone play here? They do.

Land status: Rampart Reservoir Recreation Area and Pike National Forest.

Maps: Pike National Forest; USGS Cascade.

Access: From Colorado Springs drive 18 miles west on U.S. Highway 24 toward Woodland Park. As you enter the town, turn right just before the McDonalds. Keep straight through the stop signs and past the schools. After 3 miles, turn right at Loy

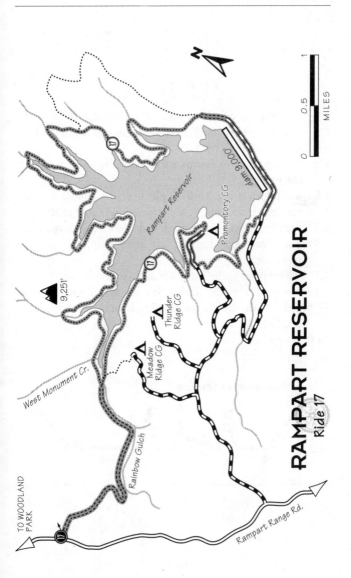

RAMPART RESERVOIR
Ride 17

Creek Road and then right again onto Rampart Range Road. Park at the Rainbow Gulch trailhead 3 miles up on the left.

The ride:

- **0.0** The Rainbow Gulch trail/road starts through the gate. Follow this downhill, keeping to the left when the road turns to doubletrack.
- **1.5** Turn right onto Rampart Reservoir Trail 700 and cross the bridge.
- **1.6** Keep left at this fork. Right leads to Meadow Ridge Campground. Simply keep toward the shore at all forks.
- **3.5** Promontory Campground. Ride down the paved road.
- **3.9** Look for the trail on the left. Take it and return to the lakeshore.
- **4.7** Paved road again. Turn left and cross the dam.
- **6.1** The road, now dirt, forks. Turn left onto the singletrack.
- **12.5** Turn right at Rainbow Gulch and return to the trailhead.
- **14.0** Trailhead.

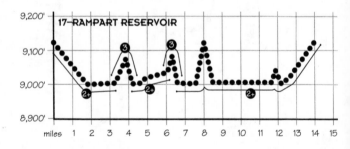

Lovell Gulch

Location: 20 miles west of Colorado Springs in Woodland Park.

Distance: 5.6-mile loop.

Time: 30 to 45 minutes.

Tread: Hard-packed dirt dominates the 4.4 miles of singletrack and 1.2 miles of doubletrack.

Aerobic level: Moderate.

Technical difficulty: 3+. A couple of sketchy downhills and an incline laced with roots and rocks warrant the plus rating.

Highlights: The singletrack winds through aspen groves, open meadows, and boulder patches while the doubletrack offers a roller-coaster downhill. Toss in wildflowers or fall colors and a backdrop of Pike's Peak and the excellent ride recipe is complete. If a pet comes along, please heed the notes at the trailhead.

Land status: Woodland Park Parks and Recreation.

Maps: Pike National Forest; USGS Mount Deception.

Access: From Colorado Springs drive about 18 miles west on U.S. Highway 24 toward Woodland Park. As you enter the town, turn right just before the McDonalds. Keep straight through the stop signs, past the schools, and bear right. 2.2 miles past McDonalds, look on the left for the animal shelter. The trailhead shares parking with the shelter.

LOVELL GULCH
Ride 18

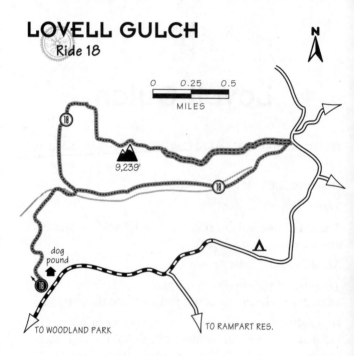

The ride:

- **0.0** Cross through the gated entry to the Lovell Trail. Don't forget to close the gate!
- **0.1** Take the right fork. If nature calls, the left fork has an answer.
- **0.2** Again, take the right fork and follow the trail markers. The spurs are closed for erosion control. When in doubt, look ahead for the next marker.

0.8 Keep some momentum as you cross the creek and turn right onto a doubletrack.

1.4 Continue straight ignoring the spur on the left.

1.7 Obey the sign and stay on the main trail. Just ahead lies a climb through boulders that may force some ratcheting.

2.5 Turn left at the gate. DO NOT go down the graded road. The route heads down the hill beneath the electrical wires.

3.7 Keep right as the doubletrack becomes faint.

4.0 Turn right. Keep an eye out for the trail marker while speeding down. Again, the markers blaze through confusion caused by erosion.

4.4 Left, over the fallen tree.

4.7 Turn right and retrace the trail.

5.6 Trailhead.

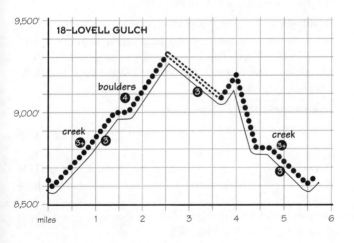

Cabin Creek

Location: Mueller State Park.

Distance: 8.4 miles out and back.

Time: 1.5 to 2.5 hours.

Tread: 8.4 miles dirt road and doubletrack.

Aerobic level: Moderate with some pretty nasty steeps.

Technical difficulty: 3. Mostly an easy technical ride with a few rutted sections. The doubletrack into Cabin Creek Pond is the most challenging part of the ride.

Highlights: The views offer up the Collegiate Peaks and the Mosquito Range while a grove of huge aspen leads into the secluded Cabin Creek Pond. The fall color change is well represented here! This ride can connect to the Dome Rock Trail (Ride 21) for a long loop.

Land status: Mueller State Park.

Maps: Mueller State Park map; USGS Divide, Cripple Creek North.

Access: From Colorado Springs drive 25 miles west on U.S. Highway 24 to Divide. Turn left at the light on Colorado Highway 67. Mueller State Park is 4 miles ahead on the right. Turn right and pay $3 at the entrance station. Continue down Wapiti Road to the Rock Pond trailhead and park.

The ride:

0.0 Rock Pond trailhead
1.2 Stay left. Brook and Rock ponds lie down the right-hand trail.
2.2 Keep left and join Four-mile Overlook Trail 44.
3.3 Turn left onto Cabin Creek Trail 45 and descend to the pond.
4.2 Cabin Creek Pond. Turn around and retrace the route. To loop with the Dome Rock Trail, continue 0.5 mile down Trail 45 and turn left onto Trail 46. To finish the loop from the Trail 46 trailhead, reverse the access directions for Ride 21 and return to the park entrance.

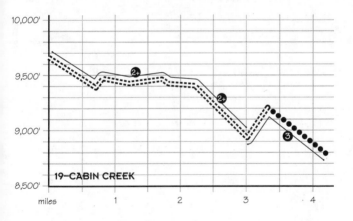

CABIN CREEK
Ride 19

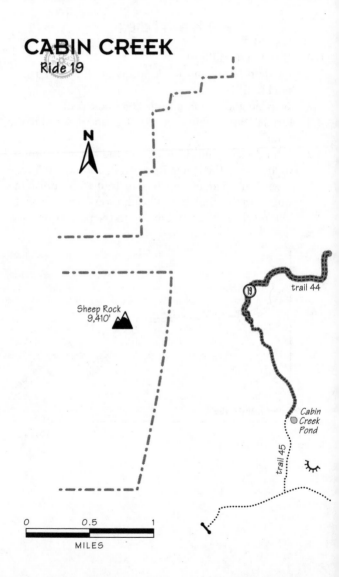

N

Sheep Rock
9,410'

19   trail 44

Cabin
Creek
Pond

trail 45

0   0.5   1
MILES

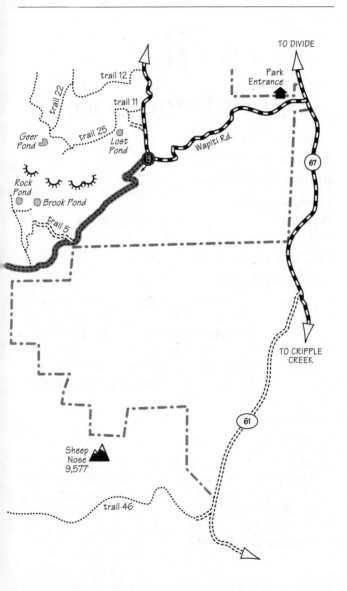

Geer Pond Loop

Location: Mueller State Park.

Distance: 10.1-mile loop.

Time: 2 hours.

Tread: 10.8 miles of single and doubletrack; 0.3 mile of paved road.

Aerobic level: Moderate.

Technical difficulty: 3.

Highlights: $3 buys a full day of pleasure on this playground's single and doubletrack. Ride through huge rock outcroppings, open meadows, tranquil ponds, and huge aspen. It's spectacular in the fall as crowds dwindle and leaves change. Occasional trail closures are updated on maps available at the park entrance and everything is well marked. The Fat Trax map shows other trails open to bikes.

Land status: Mueller State Park.

Maps: Mueller State Park recreational trails; USGS Divide.

Access: From Colorado Springs drive 25 miles west on U.S. Highway 24 to Divide. Turn left at the light on Colorado Highway 67. Mueller State Park is 4 miles ahead on the right. Turn right and pay $3 at the entrance station. Continue down Wapiti Road to the Lost Pond trailhead and park.

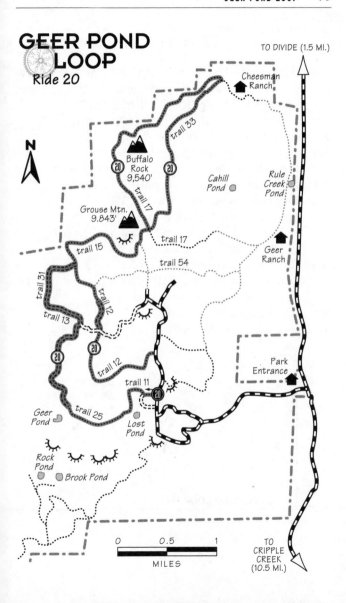

GEER POND LOOP
Ride 20

TO DIVIDE (1.5 MI.)

Cheesman Ranch

trail 33

N

Buffalo Rock 9,540'

Cahill Pond

Rule Creek Pond

trail 17

Grouse Mtn. 9,843'

trail 17

trail 15

trail 54

Geer Ranch

trail 31

trail 13

trail 12

Park Entrance

trail 12

trail 11

trail 25

Geer Pond

Lost Pond

Rock Pond

Brook Pond

0   0.5   1

MILES

TO CRIPPLE CREEK (10.5 MI.)

The ride:

0.0 Begin on the Lost Pond Trail 11. The trailhead leaves the parking lot to the west and immediately turns right.

0.5 Lost Pond. Pick up Geer Pond Trail 25.

0.9 Geer Pond. Take the left fork, staying on Trail 25.

2.1 Left on Werley Ranch Trail 13.

2.5 Right on Mountain Logger Trail 31.

3.0 Turn left on Cummings Cabin Trail 15.

4.1 Take Trail 17 left at this popular intersection.

5.2 Turn right on Buffalo Rock Trail 33.

6.5 At Cahill Pond Trail 34, turn right.

6.8 Retrace the route onto Trail 15, continuing straight on 15 where Trail 31 intersects.

8.5 Turn right on Homestead Trail 12.

8.8 Continue straight on Trail 12 as it crosses Trail 13, which leads to the campground.

9.8 Turn right on Wapiti Road.

10.1 Turn right into the trailhead parking lot.

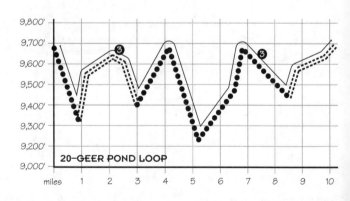

20—GEER POND LOOP

Dome Rock at Mueller State Park

Location: Mueller State Park.

Distance: 6.6 miles out and back.

Time: 45 minutes to 1 hour. Plan on a lot of sightseeing time.

Tread: 6.6 miles of good single and doubletrack. There's also about 0.1 mile spent crossing the creek nine times!

Aerobic level: Easy. A couple of the climbs may push the Easy rating. But it's mostly level.

Technical difficulty: 2+. Creek crossings and some gravel are the only real obstacles.

Highlights: A good introduction to mountain biking with the Sand Burr Mine and Jack Rabbit Lodge lying in ruin along the trail, awe-inspiring views of Dome Rock and Sheep Nose, and lots of splashing from creek crossings. Crossing Fourmile Creek feels great on hot summer days. And fall in the park is incredible!

Land status: Mueller State Park.

Maps: Mueller State Park map; USGS Cripple Creek North.

Access: From Colorado Springs drive 25 miles west on U.S. Highway 24 to Divide. Turn left at the light on Colorado Highway 67. Pass by Mueller State Park, which is 4 miles ahead on the right. 1.4 miles past the main entrance turn right on County

Road 61. Go 2 miles and turn right into the parking. Dome Rock Trail 46 is off to the right. Put $3 in the self-service permit dispenser for a day permit.

The ride:

0.0 Dome Rock Trail 46 starts in the northwest corner of the parking lot. Pass through the gate and cross the bridge.

0.5 Pass by the ruins of the Sand Burr Mine.

1.5 Stay to the right on Trail 46. The Sand Creek Trail on the left is for horse and foot traffic only.

2.3 Keep Left at Jack Rabbit Lodge. To the right, Trail 45 leads to Cabin Creek Pond and Ride 19.

3.3 The trail continues for horse and foot traffic only. Bikes are NOT allowed. Retrace the route to the trailhead.

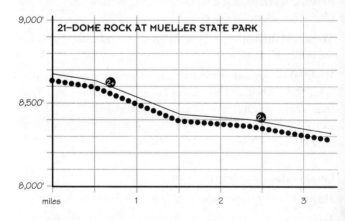

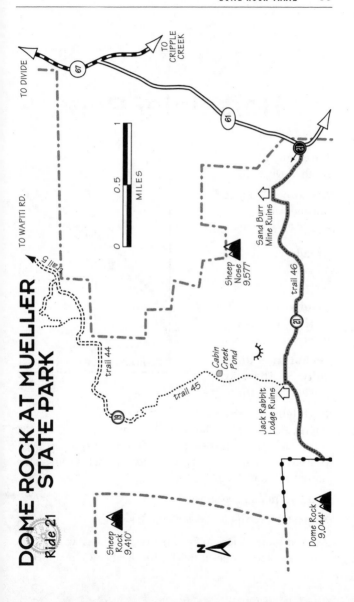

DOME ROCK AT MUELLER STATE PARK
Ride 21

TO DIVIDE

TO WAPITI RD.

67

TO CRIPPLE CREEK

61

23

trail 5

trail 44

19

trail 45

trail 46

21

Cabin Creek Pond

Jack Rabbit Lodge Ruins

Sand Burr Mine Ruins

Sheep Nose 9,577'

Sheep Rock 9,410'

Dome Rock 9,044'

N

MILES

0   0.5   1

Horsethief Park

Location: 11 miles south of Divide.

Distance: 4 miles out and back.

Time: 1 hour.

Tread: 4 miles of singletrack with a few rocky patches.

Aerobic level: Moderate. The initial climb is a doosey.

Technical difficulty: 3+. The rocky patches can be tricky.

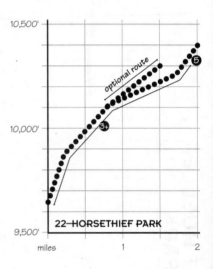

Highlights: Horse thieves are said to have holed up in the high-country park that is the backdrop of this short gem. Some traces of past occupants still remain. A loop is planned for this trail. At press-time, however, it wasn't suitable for biking.

Land status: Pike National Forest.

Maps: USGS Cripple Creek North, Pikes Peak.

Access: From Colorado Springs drive 25 miles west on U.S. Highway 24 to Divide. Turn left at the light on Colorado Highway 67. Pass by Mueller State Park. 11 miles from Divide, the road passes a closed tunnel. The tunnel's parking area is also the ride's trailhead.

The ride:

- **0.0** The trail heads up the hill from the southeast corner of the parking area.
- **0.8** Take the left fork and cross the creek. The right trail leads to Horsethief Falls and Ride 23.
- **1.7** Go left at this fork. To the right, the trail runs 0.5 mile before becoming a cairn-marked portage.
- **2.0** End of the trail.

Pancake Rocks

Location: 11 miles south of Divide.

Distance: 5.6 miles out and back.

Time: 1.5 to 2 hours.

Tread: 5.6 miles of singletrack. Roots, tight switchbacks, drop-offs, and erosion show up throughout the ride.

Aerobic level: Strenuous. A lot of climbing in a short distance.

Technical difficulty: 4. The obstacles alone aren't too bad, but pair 'em with the steeps and it's challenging.

Highlights: The Pancake Rocks are just that—rocks that look like pancakes. Getting there provides some genuine singletrack challenge through classic mountain terrain. Horsethief Falls are easily accessed and deserve a look.

Land status: Pike National Forest.

Maps: Pike National Forest; USGS Cripple Creek North, Pikes Peak.

Access: From Colorado Springs drive 25 miles west on U.S. Highway 24 to Divide. Turn left at the light on Colorado Highway 67. Pass by Mueller State Park. 11 miles from Divide, the road passes a closed tunnel. The tunnel's parking area is the ride's trailhead.

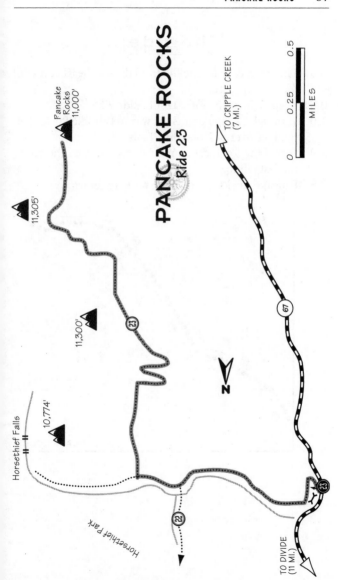

PANCAKE ROCKS
Ride 23

Pancake
Rocks
11,000'

11,305'

11,300'

10,774'

Horsethief Falls

Horsethief Park

23

23

22

67

N

TO CRIPPLE CREEK
(7 MI.)

TO DIVIDE
(11 MI.)

MILES

0   0.25   0.5

The ride:

0.0 The trail heads up the hill from the southeast corner of the parking area.

0.8 Keep right at the fork. Left is Ride 22.

1.0 Turn right. A sign points the way to Pancake Rocks. Left rambles over to Horsethief Falls.

1.9 Top of the toughest climb. Contour around the hill to the last climb.

2.8 Pancake Rocks. Retrace the route to return.

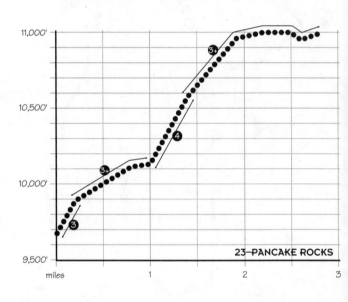

The Crags

Location: 6 miles south of Divide.

Distance: 4.2 miles out and back.

Time: 1 hour.

Tread: 4.2 miles of singletrack. Roots and gravel show up near the end of the trail.

Aerobic level: Moderate.

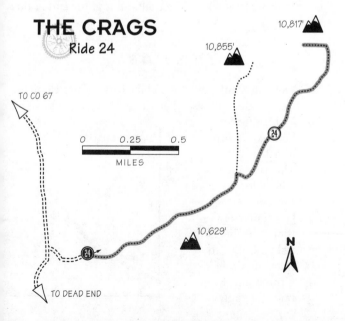

Technical difficulty: 4. While the beginning of the trail rates a 3, the last stretch gets the 4.

Highlights: Wild rock formations highlight this ride. Views of Pike's Peak and the Catamount reservoirs are also worth the trip. To make a longer and harder ride, start at the highway. An early start may help avoid crowds.

Land status: Pike National Forest.

Maps: Pike National Forest; USGS Pike's Peak, Woodland Park.

Access: From Colorado Springs drive 25 miles west on U.S. Highway 24 to Divide. Turn left at the light onto Colorado Highway 67. Drive just over 4 miles and turn left on a dirt road marked by signs for The Crags Campground and Rocky Mountain Mennonite Camp. The road is rough but passable with caution. Follow the signs to The Crags for 1.5 miles then turn left into the campground. The trailhead is at the end of this road.

The ride:

0.0 From the southeast corner of the parking area climb the steps to the trailhead. The Crags Trail goes left.

1.0 Right at the fork. Left is an optional route.

1.9 The trail bears left before the summit.

2.1 Going much further becomes risky both to rider and the environment. Retrace the route.

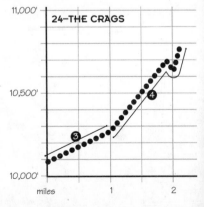

Canon City

Canon City (it's pronounced "canyon") lies 45 miles south-west of The Springs. Take Colorado Highway 115 south to Penrose. Turn right onto westbound U.S. Highway 50, which turns into Royal Gorge Boulevard upon entering the city.

To reach Cottonwood Park, and the trailhead for rides 27 and 28, turn left from Royal Gorge Boulevard onto 4th Street. The park is on the right.

Canon City offers all the amenities of a big city with a small town flavor. The few bike shops are well stocked and have mechanics. Since this is a small town, expect the stores to close early.

Oak Creek Loop

Location: 12 miles south of Canon City.

Distance: 14.6-mile loop.

Time: 2 hours.

Tread: 2.7 miles of singletrack and 11.9 miles of dirt road.

Aerobic level: Strenuous at first, gaining more than 1,200 feet in the first 2.7 miles. Moderate and mostly downhill from there.

Technical difficulty: 3. The singletrack gets narrow with some steep sidehills.

Highlights: This singletrack winds through a narrow, damp ravine amongst rocks and trees to burst out into a high meadow with a Sangre de Cristo backdrop. The environment is perfect for wildflowers throughout spring and summer. Descend the roller coaster-like Forest Road 304 or explore the other connecting roads. This is the best trail in the region.

Land status: San Isabel National Forest.

Maps: San Isabel National Forest; USGS Rockvale, Hardscrabble.

Access: From Royal Gorge Boulevard in Canon City, take 4th Street across the river and out of town. At about 1.5 miles look for the right-hand turn onto County Road 143. This road turns to a washboarded dirt road. Continue 12 miles and turn left into the Oak Creek Campground. The trailhead is at the end of this road.

OAK CREEK LOOP
Ride 25

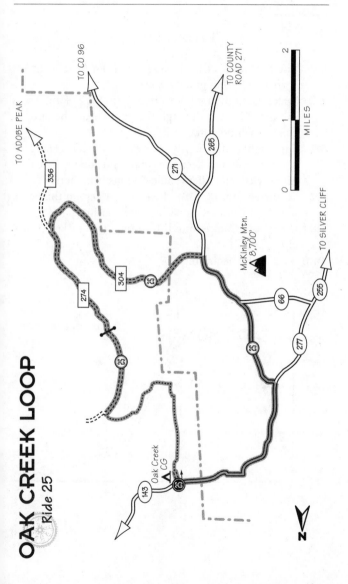

TO CO 96

TO ADOBE PEAK

336

274

304

25

25

143

Oak Creek
CG

25

271

265

TO COUNTY
ROAD 271

McKinley Mtn.
8,700

66

255

277

TO SILVER CLIFF

25

0   1   2
MILES

N

The ride:

0.0   The trail leaves the parking area from the southwest corner. Spin that granny gear!

2.7   Welcome to the top! Turn right onto FR 274 and cross the meadow. Go through the gate ahead; be sure to close it behind you.

5.7   Turn right onto FR 304 to start the descent. Hang on and remember to keep the rubber side down. The Forest Service map offers some options from here.

9.2   Turn right onto County Road 143. Keep on this main road as it descends the Oak Creek basin.

14.4 Oak Creek Campground. Turn right for one last (brief) climb.

14.6 Back at the beginning.

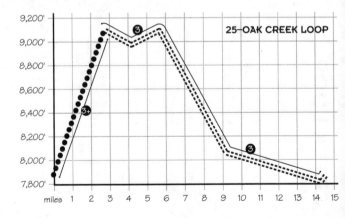

Tanner-Stultz Loop

Location: 8 miles south of Canon City.

Distance: 12.1-mile loop.

Time: 2.5 to 3 hours.

Tread: 9 miles of singletrack and 3.1 miles of dirt road. The uphill portion is littered with gravel and rocks and the downhill is like a steep, rock staircase. The middle is nice, though.

Aerobic level: Strenuous. Plenty of steep climbing!

Technical difficulty: 5+. The downhill is well-suited for a trials competition.

Highlights: With the gonzo climb to the top, the view had better be worth it! It is. The Sangre de Cristo Mountains and the Wet Mountain Valley spread out below like oil on a canvas. Wildflowers and hills lined with scrub oak make for good scenery spring, summer, and fall. The aerobic and technical workouts are very intense. Plan on some walking.

Land status: San Isabel National Forest.

Maps: San Isabel National Forest; USGS Rockvale, Curley Peak.

Access: From Royal Gorge Boulevard in Canon City, take 4th Street across the river and out of town. At 1.5 miles, just after climbing a hill, look for the right-hand turn onto County Road 143. This road turns to a washboarded dirt road. Continue 6 miles to the trailhead parking on the left. It's marked as the Tanner Trail 1334.

TANNER-STULTZ LOOP
Ride 26

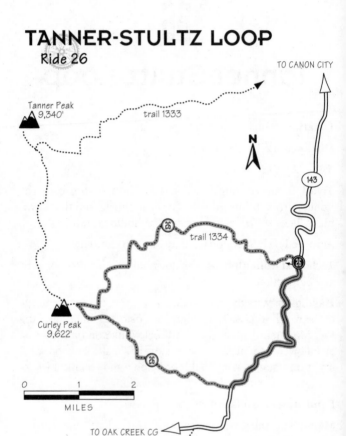

TO CANON CITY

Tanner Peak
9,340'

trail 1333

N

143

26

trail 1334

26

Curley Peak
9,622'

26

0   1   2

MILES

TO OAK CREEK CG

The ride:

0.0 Go across County Road 143 and climb onto Tanner Trail 1334. Be ready to climb hard for the first 5.5 miles.

0.9 The trail forks. Either way is workable but the one on the right is more gradual.

1.3 Take the right-hand trail at this fork for better tread.

2.8 The trail runs up a scree hill.

3.0 Go straight across this intersection.

3.6 Pick a path around the fallen tree.

4.0 The tread improves but we're still climbing.

5.3 A secondary trail cuts left, a short cut. This description stays right.

5.5 Keep left and head down East Bear Gulch. A sign points to Road 143. This is Trail 1333.

6.7 The surf is starting to rise! The first obstacle is a fallen tree; boulders, dropoffs, and switchbacks follow.

9.0 Turn left on County Road 143.

12.1 Back at the car.

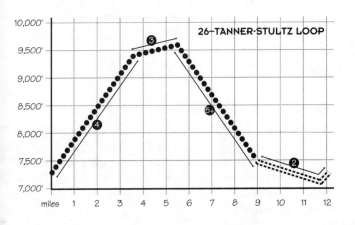

Grape Creek

Location: Canon City.

Distance: 18 miles out and back.

Time: 2.5 hours.

Tread: 6 miles of singletrack, 9.4 miles of dirt road, and 2.6 miles of paved road. The singletrack gets pretty rugged. Watch for cactus!

Aerobic level: Moderate.

Technical difficulty: 3+. The road portion of the ride rates a 2.

Highlights: This singletrack wanders along Grape Creek for a good look at an arid canyon and the remains of the old railway to Westcliffe. This trail is open most of the year, but heavy snows or high runoff can shorten the season. Park in Temple Canyon Park to ride just the singletrack. Watch for rattlesnakes and cactus.

Land status: Bureau of Land Management and Temple Canyon Park.

Maps: San Isabel National Forest; USGS Royal Gorge.

Access: This ride begins on the southwest edge of Canon City. Visitors can park in Cottonwood Park. Reach the park from Royal Gorge Boulevard by crossing the Arkansas River via 1st or 4th Street. The park lies between these two streets. To ride only the singletrack, follow ride directions to mile 6.0 and park near the restrooms.

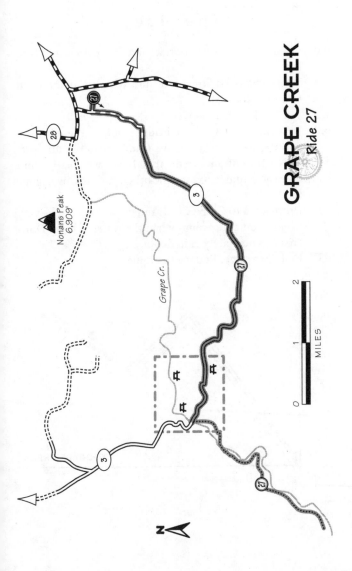

GRAPE CREEK
Ride 27

The ride:

0.0   From Cottonwood Park ride west to 1st Street and turn left.

0.8   Turn right as 1st Street runs into Temple Canyon Road (County Road 3).

1.3   The road turns to gravel.

6.0   Descending toward the bridge, look to the left for a parking area, directly across from a modern outhouse. This is the entrance to the trail. It isn't well marked but it's easy to find. Crossing the bridge means you've gone too far.

7.0   Drop down to Grape Creek and cross. This can be very tricky (and dangerous) when the water is high. Don't cross if your safety is in doubt.

9.0   End of the line. Retrace the route.

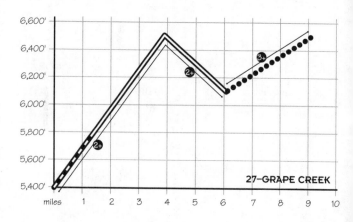

27–GRAPE CREEK

Skyline Drive

Location: Canon City.

Distance: 7.6-mile loop.

Time: 1 hour.

Tread: 7.6 miles of paved road.

Aerobic level: Moderate. The climb is fairly constant for 5 miles.

Technical difficulty: 1. The only difficulties are with vehicular traffic.

Highlights: The bird's eye views of Canon City and the state penitentiary are grand from this prisoner-built road. This is a good workout with a fun downhill portion. However, it is very exposed both to the sun and cars. Be careful on both accounts.

Land status: Various public and private holdings.

Maps: San Isabel National Forest; Canon City street map; USGS Royal Gorge, Canon City.

Access: This ride begins in Canon City. Park in Cottonwood Park. From Royal Gorge Boulevard (US 50) you can reach the park by crossing the Arkansas River via 1st or 4th Street. Parking is available throughout the park. The odometer readings below begin from the parking lot near the tennis courts.

The ride:

0.0   Exit the park by turning right on 2nd Street. Then turn left onto Riverside.

0.2   Turn right onto 1st Street.

0.4   Turn left onto Royal Gorge Boulevard (US 50). Ride on the right shoulder. It narrows around the bend but soon widens.

3.4   Turn right and enter Skyline Drive.

5.5   The top. Now you know why Canon is pronounced *canyon*. Enjoy the downhill that follows.

6.1   Turn right onto 5th Street.

6.8   Turn right on Royal Gorge Boulevard.

7.0   Turn left on 4th Street.

7.3   Go right on Griffin Avenue and into Cottonwood Park.

7.6   Back at the car.

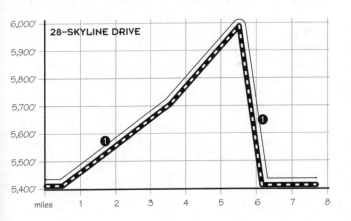

San Isabel Lake

San Isabel Lake is a 40-acre reservoir nestled in the Wet Mountains about 75 miles southwest of Colorado Springs. From Colorado Springs drive 35 miles southwest on Colorado Highway 115 through Penrose and into Florence. Turn left and drive 11 miles south to Wetmore on CO 67. Turn right onto CO 96 and climb up and over Hardscrabble Pass 10 miles to McKenzie Junction. Turn left onto CO 165 and drive 18 miles south to the lake.

San Isabel Lake offers only limited lodging. Camping, however, is fairly plentiful with Ophir Creek, Davenport, and San Isabel campgrounds. Supplies are sparse. It's wise to bring all you'll need with you and gas up the car in Florence.

A truly unique site in the area is the Bishop Castle. It is on CO 165 about 10 miles north of the lake. Jim Bishop is building the castle by hand. It is free to visit, but he is funding it solely from sightseers' donations.

Snowslide Trail

Location: About 45 miles south of Canon City; 0.4 mile south of San Isabel Lake.

Distance: 5.2 miles one way.

Time: 1.5 hours.

Tread: 5.2 miles of singletrack.

Aerobic level: Strenuous; steep, but not too long.

Technical difficulty: 4. Erosion on the steeps has created some rough going.

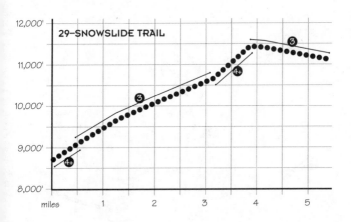

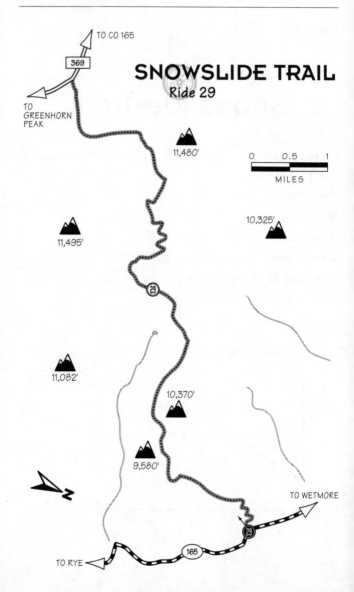

TO CO 165

369

SNOWSLIDE TRAIL
Ride 29

TO
GREENHORN
PEAK

11,480'

0   0.5   1
MILES

11,495'

10,325'

29

11,082'

10,370'

9,580'

N

TO WETMORE

29

165

TO RYE

Highlights: Views include Pueblo Reservoir, the old Pueblo steel mill, and the Sangre de Cristo Mountains. The challenging singletrack is steep and technical as it winds up through raw and unspoiled forest. Link this trail with the Cisneros Trail (see Ride 30) for a loop with a good downhill run.

Land status: San Isabel National Forest.

Maps: San Isabel National Forest; USGS San Isabel.

Access: From San Isabel Lake drive 0.4 mile south on Colorado Highway 165. The Snowslide Trail sign is on the right. A pull-off parking area is on the left.

The ride:

0.0 The trail jumps straight into the woods and becomes steep and technical.
0.5 The tread grows smoother and a bit less steep.
3.1 Switchbacks. And you thought it was steep before!
3.8 Finally! The climb ends.
4.0 Start down to the road.
5.2 Greenhorn Road. Turn around and retrace your tracks, or go right to the Cisneros Trail (Ride 30).

30

Cisneros Trail

Location: San Isabel Lake.

Distance: 7.6 miles one way.

Time: 2 hours up and 45 minutes down.

Tread: 5.9 miles of singletrack, 0.5 mile of gravel road, and 1.2 miles of paved road.

Aerobic level: Moderate. The steeps are strenuous but spread out a bit.

Technical difficulty: 3+.

Highlights: The initial granny gear climb gives access to gorgeous meadows and an old mine's spur trail. Snowmobilers use the upper region in the winter. Following their blazes (orange diamonds) will lead you astray. But if you get off track, those same blazes will lead you to Greenhorn Road, where a left sends you to the upper trailhead. For a loop with the Snowslide Trail (Ride 29), the Cisneros Trail is the more gradual climb of the two.

Land status: San Isabel National Forest.

Maps: San Isabel National Forest; USGS San Isabel.

Access: This ride begins at San Isabel Lake. The odometer readings start at the south entrance to the recreational area just past mile marker 19 on Colorado Highway 165. Parking is available 0.2 mile north of the entrance on the highway or in numerous places within the recreational area.

The ride:

0.0   During fall, a gate closes the south entrance of the recreational area to cars. Keep to the main road, avoiding the picnic and camping areas. There is an area map on the right side of the road.

1.2   As the main road starts to bend right, turn left toward the Cisneros Trail and follow the signs.

1.7   Keep following the signs; make a left followed by a right.

CISNEROS TRAIL
Ride 30

- **2.0** This is the Cisneros trailhead with parking available. Head up the singletrack.
- **2.4** Keep right. A trail from the group camping area joins here.
- **2.9** Keep left as the St. Charles Trail (Ride 31) peels off to the right.
- **3.4** Keep left. This spur heads to the Marion mine ruins.
- **5.3** Cross Amethyst Creek.
- **5.4** Turn left at this fork. Right follows a snowmobile trail to Greenhorn Mountain Road.
- **5.8** Cross the St. Charles River. No, it doesn't look like a river.
- **7.6** Greenhorn Mountain Road. Turn around to reap your rewards, or turn left to complete a loop with Snowslide Trail (see Ride 29).

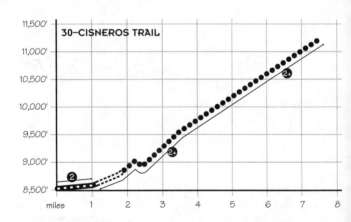

St. Charles Peak

Location: San Isabel Lake.

Distance: 15-mile loop.

Time: 3.5 hours.

Tread: 9.6 miles of singletrack and 5.4 miles of paved road. Some swampy conditions may exist around the 5-mile mark and loose gravel shows up on the steeps.

Aerobic level: Strenuous. Steeps in excess of 1,000 feet per mile on this one!

Technical difficulty: 4. Steep, tight switchbacks make for an interesting descent.

Highlights: The feeling of accomplishment is almost as great as the views from climbing St. Chuck. This major-league workout and technical test is surrounded by beauty on par with the rest of the area. Take your time and enjoy the sights.

Land status: San Isabel National Forest.

Maps: San Isabel National Forest; USGS San Isabel, St. Charles Peak.

Access: This ride begins at San Isabel Lake. The odometer readings start at the south entrance to the recreational area just past mile marker 19 on Colorado Highway 165. Parking is available 0.2 mile north of the entrance on the highway or in numerous places within the recreational area. In the fall, a gate closes the entrance to cars.

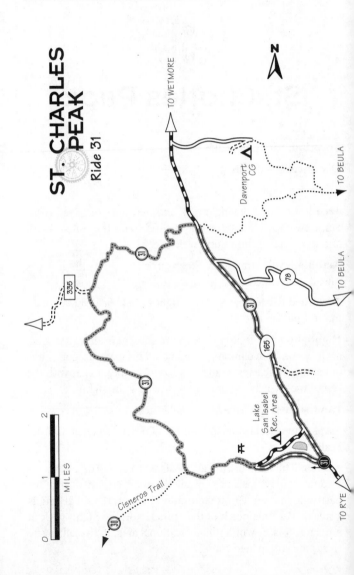

ST. CHARLES PEAK
Ride 31

TO WETMORE

N

Davenport CG

TO BEULA

335

31

78

TO BEULA

31

165

Lake
San Isabel
Rec. Area

MILES
0   1   2

31

Cisneros Trail

30

TO RYE

The ride:

0.0 Start at the south entrance to the recreational area. Keep to the main road, avoiding the picnic and camping areas.

1.2 As the main road starts to bend right, turn left toward the Cisneros Trail and follow the signs.

1.7 Keep following the signs; make a left followed by a right.

2.0 This is the Cisneros trailhead with parking available. Head up the singletrack.

2.4 Keep right. A trail from the group camping area joins here.

2.9 Turn right and head up the St. Charles Trail.

4.0 Catch a glimpse of Lake Marion to the left as the climb levels out and the track becomes swampy.

5.6 Keep right as Forest Road 335 intersects the trail. FR 335 leads down to Greenhorn Road.

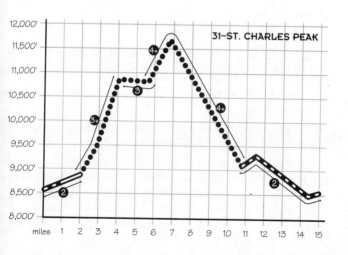

6.8 Contour around the summit and begin to head down. Many tight switchbacks lie ahead.

10.8 Turn right on CO 165. A brief climb, then more downhill.

11.5 Keep on the main road as CO 78 joins from the left.

14.4 Pass by San Isabel Lake.

15.0 Back at the beginning.

Squirrel Creek

Location: 6 miles north of San Isabel Lake.

Distance: 4.2 miles out and back.

Time: 1 hour.

Tread: 4.2 miles of singletrack.

Aerobic level: Moderate. This is the most gradual of the region's trails and we're pointed downhill all the way.

Technical difficulty: 4. The trail mingles with the creek and a boulder field.

Highlights: This ride offers a fun descent through a variety of creek environments. It starts in an open valley, then twists into a narrow, rocky gorge, and ends above an arid canyon. Technical challenges range from numerous creek crossings to a large boulder field. Keep your eyes peeled for wildlife. I saw a mountain lion in the canyon. The trail can be used as a downhill, a shuttle ride to Beulah, or as a link to the Lion Park Trail. While

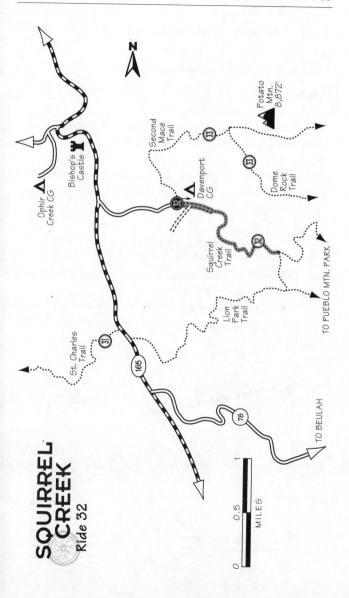

SQUIRREL CREEK
Ride 32

N

Ophir Creek CG

Bishop's Castle

Second Mace Trail

Potato Mtn. 8,872'

Davenport CG

32

33

33

Dome Rock Trail

32

Squirrel Creek Trail

Lion Park Trail

TO PUEBLO MTN. PARK

St. Charles Trail

31

165

78

TO BEULAH

0   0.5   1
MILES

Lion Park would be a strenuous climb, the downhill is aerobically easy.

Land status: San Isabel National Forest.

Maps: San Isabel National Forest; USGS St. Charles Peak.

Access: The Davenport Campground serves as the launching point for this ride. From San Isabel Lake drive about 6 miles north on Colorado Highway 165. Turn right on Forest Road 382 at the Davenport Campground sign. Drive 1.3 miles down this dirt road. On the left is an old, brick chimney. This is the trailhead. This also makes an excellent shuttle ride by parking a car in Beulah.

The ride:

0.0 Descend FR 382 into the Davenport Campground. Stay on the main campground road.

0.2 As the road sweeps right, keep straight and start down the Squirrel Creek Trail. A large sign marks the trailhead.

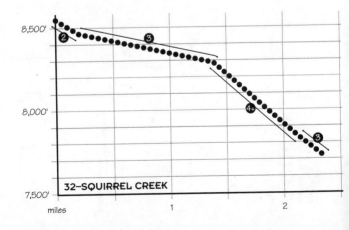

32—SQUIRREL CREEK

0.4 This is the first of nine creek crossings. This one is pretty smooth, but they get progressively more technical.

1.4 An old cement wall lies along the creek.

1.6 This boulder field gets a tech rating of 5+. An excellent rider may be able to descend it, but only the superhuman will be able to climb this stretch. Another old wall is a short distance downstream from here.

1.8 This creek crossing can be very slick.

2.0 The trail finally smooths out. A very faint trail to the right leads to Lion Park.

2.1 An old foundation zips by on the right.

2.3 The trail widens, skirting the canyon's rim and an old wooden railing. Turn around before you make the return trip too long. Continuing downhill leads to Pueblo Mountain Park and Beulah.

Second Mace–
Dome Rock

Location: 6 miles north of San Isabel Lake.

Distance: 25.7-mile loop.

Time: 5 hours.

Tread: 8.3 miles of singletrack, 12.1 miles of dirt road, and 5.3 miles of paved road.

Aerobic level: Strenuous. It can be shortened to create a moderate ride.

Technical difficulty: 4+. The trip to Dome Rock rates a 3+ with the main difficulties following.

Highlights: Dome Rock is an impressive blob of rock overlooking a rugged canyon. Some folks may want to turn around after the moderate trip to the rock, rather than tackling the long, technical downhill and 10-mile climb that follows. Use a shuttle to make this terrific technical test all downhill.

Land status: San Isabel National Forest.

Maps: San Isabel National Forest.

Access: The Davenport Campground serves as the launching point for this ride. From San Isabel Lake drive about 6 miles north on Colorado Highway 165. Turn right on Forest Road 382 at the Davenport Campground sign. Drive 1.3 miles down this dirt road. On the left is an old, brick chimney. This is the

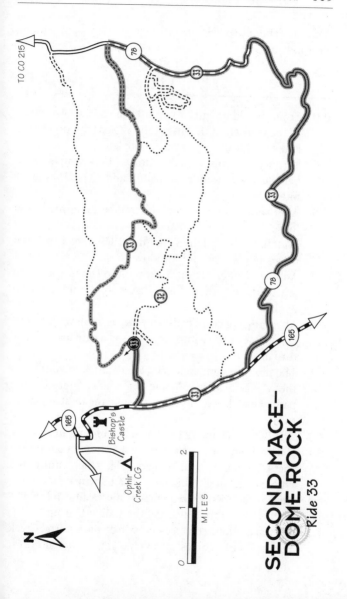

SECOND MACE—
DOME ROCK
Ride 33

TO CO 215

78

33

33

33

32

33

78

165

165

Bishop's
Castle

Ophir
Creek CG

N

MILES
0 1 2

trailhead. This also makes an excellent shuttle ride by parking a car in Beulah.

The ride:

0.0 From the chimney, head uphill. The trail proper starts to the rear left of the little valley. Cross the tiny brook and switchback up the hill to the left.

1.0 Turn right at this T intersection. A broken-up sign labels Beulah as 6 miles downhill and CO 160 as left 1 mile.

1.5 After some rolling terrain, the trail becomes rocky and loose.

1.7 Watch out for a fallen tree here. Up ahead the trail bursts into a beautiful meadow.

2.4 Another T intersection. Turn right to Dome Rock. The left trail continues above Dome Rock and down to Beulah.

4.2 After crossing creek beds a few times, both wet and dry, Dome Rock comes into view. This is where many riders turn around.

4.6 The trail gets a bit confusing after a brief downhill into the woods. A large root and some fallen limbs bar the path ahead. Heed this hint and take the tight left-hand turn.

4.7 The base of Dome Rock. The point of no return.

5.1 The tech-level has just risen to a 5. It will continue in the 4-5 category for almost a mile. When confronted with a confusing trail choice, head downstream.

6.1 The creek-crossing frequency is increasing and they're often wet. On the plus side, the trail fattens up.

7.2 After about fourteen creek crossings, the Squirrel Creek Picnic Shelter comes into view. This National Forest

Historical Site was one of the Forest Service's first recreational facilities, originally built in 1919.

7.8   After seven more creek crossings, turn left at this trail junction down toward Beulah.

8.3   The trail becomes doubletrack, then a dirt road. Follow this downhill into Beulah.

10.0 Turn right at a 4-way intersection. Stay on the main road.

11.1 Turn left at the T junction, then immediately turn right onto Pine Drive (CO 78).

12.3 Stay on CO 78 as it winds up past Pueblo Mountain Park. It turns to dirt after 1 mile and continues on a long, constant climb.

22.2 Turn right onto CO 165.

22.9 Pass by the Lion's Park and St. Charles trailheads.

24.4 Turn right down FR 382 and descend into the Davenport Campground.

25.7 Collapse at the car.

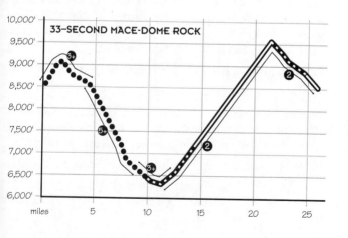

Deer Peak

Location: 8 miles north of San Isabel Lake.

Distance: 18.2-mile loop.

Time: 4 hours.

Tread: 16.1 miles of dirt road and 2.1 miles of extremely rough four-wheel-drive road with boulders a'plenty.

Aerobic level: Strenuous.

Technical difficulty: 4. The four-wheel-drive road is boulder-strewn and steep.

Highlights: This is an extreme workout NOT for the faint-hearted! Deer Peak does offer unobstructed views and some wildlife is bound to scamper by during the climb. The last stretch of downhill is through an old mining district. Traces of prospect holes and mines litter the roadside.

Land status: San Isabel National Forest and private holdings.

Maps: San Isabel National Forest; USGS Deer Peak.

Access: From San Isabel Lake drive 7 miles north on Colorado Highway 165. Turn left at the Ophir Creek Campground sign onto Forest Road 360. Continue over the cattle guard and up the road. At the 0.2-mile point FR 364 peels off to the right. Park and ride.

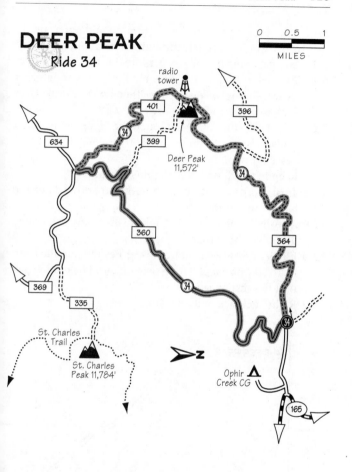

DEER PEAK
Ride 34

radio
tower

401

396

634

34

399

Deer Peak
11,572'

34

360

364

34

369

335

St. Charles
Trail

St. Charles
Peak 11,784'

N

34

Ophir
Creek CG

165

The ride:

0.0 Ride up FR 364 to the east.

1.1 Keep straight on the main road.

2.4 Bear right onto FR 396.

3.1 After passing an old shack, turn left and left again. In other words, keep left through the entire intersection.

3.4 Two sweeping hairpin corners are due up anytime now.

6.1 Turn left onto FR 401. This road gets very rough as it weaves through a logging area then up Deer Peak. Deer Peak is the one with the towers on it.

8.2 Deer Peak summit. Don't touch the equipment! When ready to leave, continue on FR 401. FR 399 is a rougher descent option from here.

8.7 Keep left each time a road joins this one.

11.3 Turn left onto FR 360. The other road heads to the hamlet of Gardner.

11.9 A tornado once tore through this region. A sign here describes the carnage.

12.5 FR 399 has descended from Deer Peak to join the main road. Stay on FR 360 from here on out. The mining district lies just ahead.

18.2 Right back where it all started.

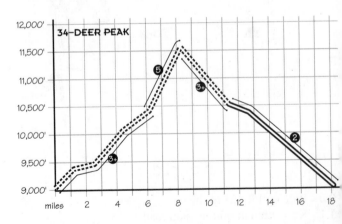

Junkins Park Loop

Location: 15 miles north of San Isabel Lake and 18 miles east of Westcliffe.

Distance: 17-mile loop.

Time: 2.5 hours.

Tread: 14.8 miles of dirt road and 4 miles of paved road.

Aerobic level: Moderate. The first 9 miles climb gradually.

Technical difficulty: 2.

Highlights: This picturesque ride doesn't require any special technical abilities. The initial ascent parallels a brook that runs amongst boulder outcroppings and aspens. Check out the domesticated elk ranch as the road levels out, then pedal through Junkins Park. The Sangre de Cristo views and rapid descent just add to the fun.

Land status: San Isabel National Forest and private holdings.

Maps: San Isabel National Forest; USGS Hardscrabble, Rosita, Deer Peak.

Access: From San Isabel Lake drive 15 miles north on Colorado Highway 165 to McKenzie Junction and turn left on CO 96. The next left is County Road 358. This is the trailhead. Drive up the road a bit and park. 4 miles up CO 96 is an alternate trailhead where Rosita Road (CR 347) meets the highway.

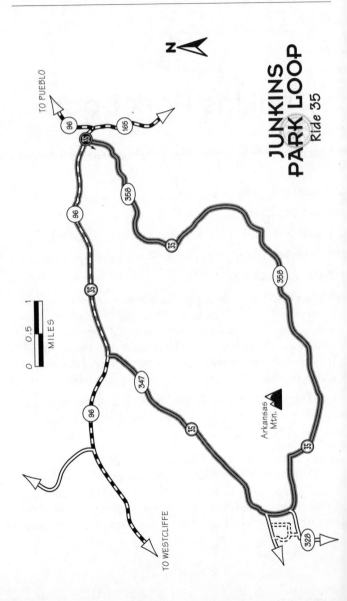

The ride:

0.0   Head away from CO 96 on County Road 358.
0.9   Cross the cattle guard.
5.3   An elk ranch passes by on the left.
9.1   Leave Junkins Park via a fast and fun descent.
10.1 Turn right, then keep right onto Rosita Road (CR 347).
14.8 Turn right on CO 96. This is the alternate trailhead.
18.8 Back at CR 358.

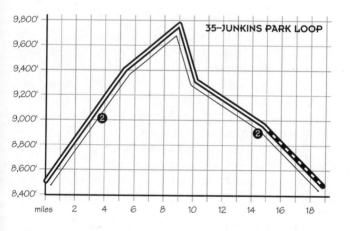

Wet Mountain Valley – Sangre de Cristo Mountains

Westcliffe, 75 miles southwest of Colorado Springs, is the main town in the sparsely populated Wet Mountain Valley. From Colorado Springs drive 35 miles southwest on Colorado Highway 115 through Penrose to Florence. Turn left and take CO 67 11 miles south to Wetmore. Turn right onto CO 96 and drive 27 miles west to Silver Cliff. Westcliffe is 2 miles farther west on CO 96 at the junction with CO 69.

Westcliffe and Silver Cliff offer some quaint lodging along with nearby camping. Groceries and supplies are plentiful, but biking gear is hard to come by. Ask around if you need something. The natives are quite friendly and will do their best to help out.

The region is ripe with history. Silver Cliff was nearly selected as Colorado's capital when it was a large, influential silver community. In this century, its graveyard was made famous in *National Geographic* for unexplained "ghost lights."

Numerous other settlements once thrived in the area including a German colony and Spanish Conquistadors! The book store in Westcliffe and the museum in Silver Cliff are great places to uncover more information.

Ghost Town Loop

Location: 7 miles east of Westcliffe.

Distance: 12.8-mile loop.

Time: 1.5 hours.

Tread: 12.8 miles of dirt road.

Aerobic level: Moderate.

Technical difficulty: 2. A couple of soft shoulders and an occasional car are the main obstacles.

Highlights: Ride through two ghost towns and past numerous old mines. Rosita was a thriving town complete with a brewery, and Querida once boasted a population of 10,000. Old mines, such as the Bassik on Mount Tyndall, produced ore rich in silver and occasionally gold. Keep an eye out for the local elk and deer herds.

Land status: Bureau of Land Management and private holdings.

Maps: San Isabel National Forest; USGS Mount Tyndall, Rosita.

Access: From Westcliffe drive 7.5 miles east on Colorado Highway 96 to County Road 341. Park beside the road.

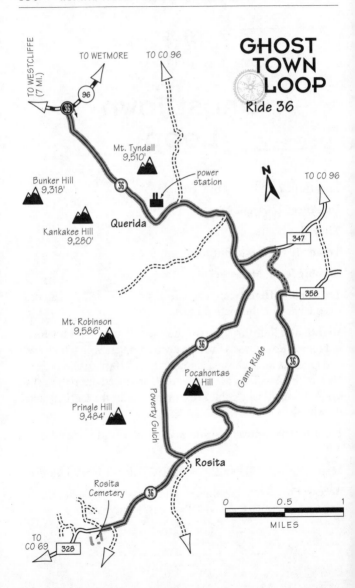

TO WESTCLIFFE (7 Mi.)

TO WETMORE

TO CO 96

GHOST TOWN LOOP
Ride 36

96

36

Mt. Tyndall
9,510'

power station

Bunker Hill
9,318'

Querida

N

TO CO 96

Kankakee Hill
9,280'

347

358

Mt. Robinson
9,586'

36

Pocahontas Hill

Game Ridge

36

Pringle Hill
9,484'

Poverty Gulch

Rosita

Rosita Cemetery

36

TO CO 69

328

0   0.5   1

MILES

The ride:

0.0 Ride up CR 341.

1.3 Welcome to downtown Querida. The chimney on the left is the remains of the old assay office. Mount Tyndall is on the left with the Bassik mine on top.

1.5 Keep right and stay on CR 341. The road to the left is closed to vehicular traffic.

2.4 At the bottom of the hill, turn right onto CR 329.

4.4 Descend through Poverty Gulch into Rosita. Turn right onto CR 328.

5.9 The Rosita Cemetery. Turn around here and retrace your tracks to the junction with CR 329 (see mile 4.4 above).

7.4 Continue straight on CR 328 and climb along Game Ridge.

9.6 Turn left onto Buttercup Lane.

10.1 Turn left onto CR 347, which soon becomes CR 341.

10.4 Continue straight, retracing the route.

12.8 Back at the car.

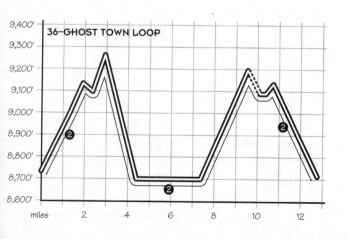

Lake DeWeese Loop

Location: 5 miles north of Westcliffe.

Distance: 12.8-mile loop.

Time: 1 hour.

Tread: 8.4 miles of dirt road and 4.4 miles of paved road.

Aerobic level: Moderate. Length will be the main challenge for beginners.

Technical difficulty: A 2- road ride. But the first mile has a couple of 2+ spots.

Highlights: Keep company with the Sangre de Cristo mountains on this level ride as the road loops around DeWeese Reservoir. Abundant waterfowl call this refuge home. The campground here makes a good base of operations when vis-

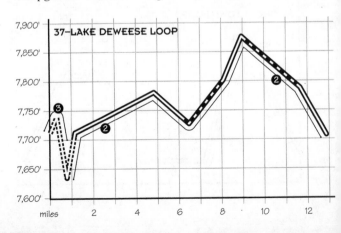

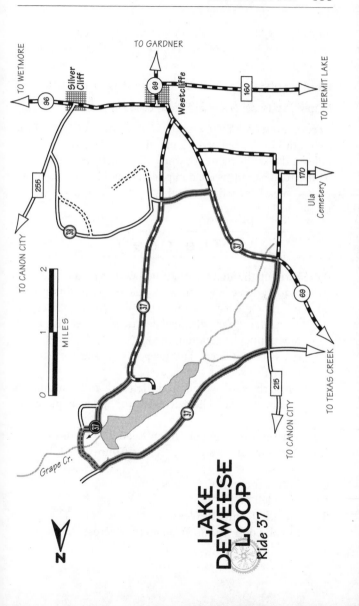

TO WETMORE

TO GARDNER

TO HERMIT LAKE

96

Silver Cliff

69

Westcliffe

160

255

38

170

Ula Cemetery

37

37

69

2

1

0

MILES

37

37

215

TO CANON CITY

TO CANON CITY

TO TEXAS CREEK

Grape Cr.

N

LAKE DEWEESE LOOP
Ride 37

iting the Wet Mountain Valley. While not a busy road, the traffic on Colorado Highway 69 isn't really expecting bikers so ride accordingly.

Land status: DeWeese Wildlife Refuge and private holdings.

Maps: San Isabel National Forest; USGS Westcliffe.

Access: From Westcliffe drive 0.3 mile north on CO 69. Turn right onto DeWeese Road (County Road 241). Drive east 4.3 miles and take the right fork where the road turns to dirt. Stay on this road past the waste dump station and down to the main parking area. The trail starts at the "modern" outhouses. Water is also available here.

The ride:

0.0   Head up through the campsites away from the lake. The roads go every which-way. Just keep climbing until reaching the main dirt road that descends to the creek.

0.2   Turn left onto the dirt road described above. This is the most difficult section of road.

0.5   Cross Grape Creek and keep left. Sometimes storms make this section rough.

1.1   Cross the cattle guard on the left fork and continue on this main road. The side roads to the left explore the lakeshore.

4.8   Turn left on Copper Gulch Road 215. Scout out St. Andrews at Westcliffe, Custer County's 9-hole golf course.

6.3   Turn left onto CO 69. Watch for cars.

8.0   Turn left on CR 243.

8.8   Turn left onto DeWeese Road (CR 241). The Sliver Streak Loop (Ride 38) enters from across the road.

11.5 Take the right fork and follow the dirt road back down to the main parking area.

12.8 Loop's completion.

Silver Streak

Location: Westcliffe.

Distance: 6.6-mile loop.

Time: 30 minutes.

Tread: 3.5 miles of dirt road and 3.1 miles of paved road.

Aerobic level: Easy.

Technical difficulty: 2.

Highlights: Fool's gold (iron pyrite) glitters in the sun as you ride through Colorado's silver mining past and among the old pulling shacks and mine tailings that still dot the countryside. Exploring the four-wheel-drive roads in the hills is a great workout aerobically and technically. These optional routes are on the map.

Land status: BLM and private holdings.

Maps: San Isabel National Forest; USGS Westcliffe.

Access: This ride begins in Westcliffe. Parking is available throughout Westcliffe. A good spot is at the Conoco station between Westcliffe and Silver Cliff, or try the school in Westcliffe.

SILVER STREAK
Ride 38

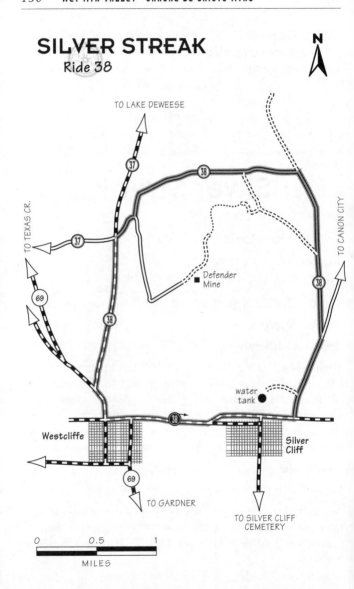

N

TO LAKE DEWEESE

TO TEXAS CR.

37

37

69

38

38

Defender Mine

TO CANON CITY

38

water tank

Westcliffe

Silver Cliff

38

69

TO GARDNER

TO SILVER CLIFF CEMETERY

0   0.5   1

MILES

The ride:

0.0 From Westcliffe head up Colorado Highway 96 toward Silver Cliff. The odometer readings start at the Custer County Bank.

1.0 Turn left onto County Road 255. The road descends briefly, crosses a cattle guard, and climbs a short hill.

1.7 Turn left onto CR 251. It is mostly level or downhill from here on out.

2.3 Keep right at this fork. Left is an easy and interesting optional trail.

3.0 Keep left here. Right leads to a trespassing situation.

4.5 Turn right then left onto paved Lake DeWeese Road, which rolls down toward Westcliffe. The optional trail here leads to the Defender mine.

6.0 Turn left onto CO 69 and descend to town.

6.3 Turn left and cruise up Main Street to your car.

6.6 Completion of the loop.

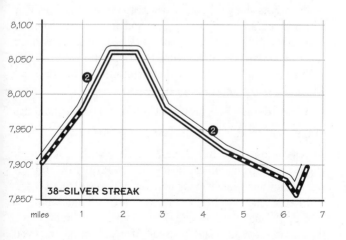

Horn Creek Loop

Location: 8 miles south of Westcliffe.

Distance: 15.9-mile loop.

Time: 2 hours.

Tread: 5.6 miles of singletrack, 5.8 miles of dirt road, and 4.5 miles of paved road.

Aerobic level: Moderate. The majority of the climbing is done on dirt and paved roads.

Technical difficulty: 3+. The singletrack section has some tight spots with a few roots and rocks tossed in.

Highlights: This scenic loop follows a leg of the Rainbow Trail as it contours along the Sangre de Cristo Mountains. The high-lake trails enter the wilderness area and are off limits to bikes. If using the Alvarado Campground as a base, this makes an excellent first day ride. To lengthen the loop, simply start pedaling in Westcliffe and follow the directions to the trailhead, where the odometer readings begin.

Land status: San Isabel National Forest and private holdings.

Maps: San Isabel National Forest; USGS Horn Peak.

Access: From Westcliffe drive 3.3 miles south on Colorado Highway 69 to Schoolfield Road (County Road 140) and turn right. Continue straight at the four-way intersection past Macey and Kettle lanes. At the T intersection turn left and follow the road up through the Alvarado Campground. The trailhead is at the end of the road. Water is usually available at the trailhead.

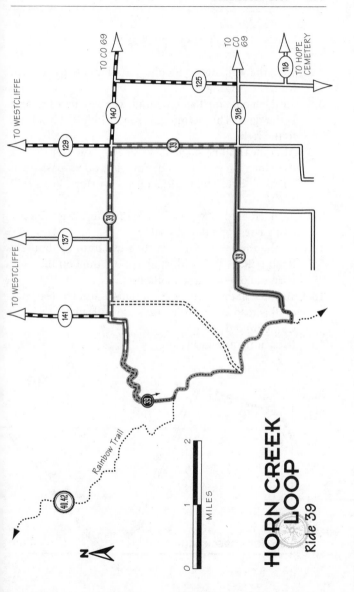

HORN CREEK LOOP
Ride 39

The ride:

0.0 Take the well-signed Rainbow Trail access path south from the parking area.

0.5 Turn left onto the Rainbow Trail. The sign here has seen better days! The Hermit Pass route (Ride 40) heads off to the right.

5.5 After the thrilling singletrack, the Rainbow Trail crosses the Horn Creek trailhead. Turn left down past Horn Creek Lodge. The trail merges with Horn Road (CR 130).

8.6 Turn left onto Macey Lane (CR 129). In Custer County this passes for a paved road.

10.6 At the four-way junction turn left onto Schoolfield Road (CR 140). The dilapidated building on the right is an old one-room schoolhouse.

13.4 Turn left at the T intersection. This is still CR 140. Stay on this road as it turns to dirt and winds up to Alvarado Campground.

15.9 Back at the trailhead.

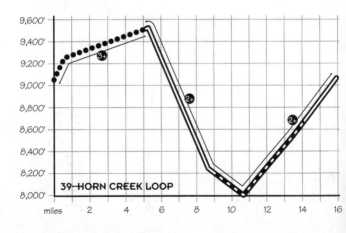

Hermit Pass

Location: 8 miles southwest of Westcliffe.

Distance: 21.9 miles out and back.

Time: 5 to 7 hours.

Tread: 9.6 miles of singletrack and 12.3 of rough four-wheel-drive road.

Aerobic level: Strenuous. The singletrack is moderate, but the next 6.1 miles of extreme climbing gives this ride a strenuous rating.

Technical difficulty: 4. The singletrack section rates a 3+, but the continuously rocky four-wheel-drive road justifies the overall rating.

Highlights: The view from above timberline is unforgettable. Add to that four high-country lakes; the Wet Mountain Valley below; a spur to Hermit Lake; beaver ponds; abundant wildlife; wildflowers galore. It all combines to make this the ultimate trail in the region. When I last rode this loop, snow blocked the final 0.1 or 0.2 mile of the road. This was in August following a heavy-snow winter.

Land status: San Isabel National Forest.

Maps: San Isabel National Forest; USGS Horn Peak.

Access: From Westcliffe drive 3.3 miles south on Colorado Highway 69 to Schoolfield Road (County Road 140) and turn right. Continue straight at the four-way intersection past Macey

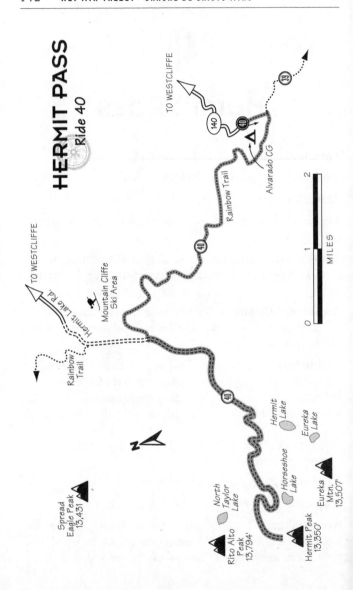

HERMIT PASS
Ride 40

TO WESTCLIFFE

TO WESTCLIFFE

Hermit Lake Rd.

Rainbow Trail

Mountain Cliffe Ski Area

Rainbow Trail

Alvarado CG

Spread Eagle Peak 13,431'

Rito Alto Peak 13,794'

North Taylor Lake

Hermit Peak 13,350'

Horseshoe Lake

Hermit Lake

Eureka Lake

Eureka Mtn. 13,507'

N

0   1   2

MILES

and Kettle lanes. At the T intersection turn left and follow the road up through Alvarado Campground. Keep on the campground road all the way to its end (about 0.8 mile), then park. The trail is marked by a large sign and leaves the parking area to the south. There is a water spigot on the northeast side of the parking area.

The ride:

0.0 The first couple hundred yards are actually cemented singletrack. The trail angles south then, and after a couple of switchbacks and a light climb, hits the Rainbow Trail.

0.5 Rainbow Trail. An abused sign marks this trail. Turn right and enjoy the smooth trail. Keep on the Rainbow Trail until it runs into Hermit Lake Road. En route ride past the Comanche, Venable, and Goodwin trails. The gradual climb on the well-marked Rainbow is occasionally rocky.

4.8 Hermit Lake Road and the Hermit Beaver Ponds. Cross the bridge on the Rainbow and turn left onto the road. Take note of the sign "Some roads closed due to...."

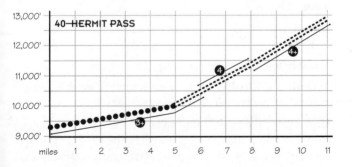

This will help you locate the trail on the return trip. Missing the turn means using the valley road system to complete the loop.

8.0 Hermit Lake trailhead. Keep on the road. The trail is a nice side-trip of about 0.25 mile down to the lake. Then prepare for 3 miles of steep climbs and rocky road to the top of Hermit Pass.

11.0 Top of Hermit Pass. Enjoy the view! Retrace the route for the return trip. The extremely rocky road can be tricky on the downhill. Stop to rest as needed to recover arm strength.

South Colony

Location: 13 miles south of Westcliffe.

Distance: 12.8 miles out and back.

Time: 3 hours.

Tread: 12.8 miles of four-wheel-drive road. The first mile is VERY rough.

Aerobic level: Strenuous. Up, up, up, and more up!

Technical difficulty: 4. The smooth patches are fine. But the road takes no prisoners when it gets rough!

Highlights: Making it to the top (at 11,300 feet) is the biggest highlight and a true accomplishment. The road's end is surrounded by five 14,000-foot peaks. The Crestone Needle, third

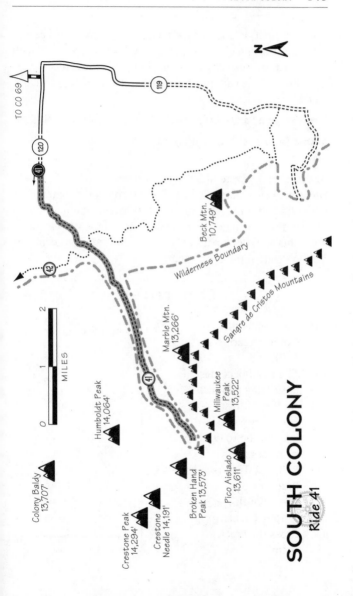

N

TO CO 69

119

120

41

42

Beck Mtn.
10,749'

Wilderness Boundary

Marble Mtn.
13,266'

Sangre de Cristos Mountains

Humboldt Peak
14,064'

41

Miliwaukee
Peak
13,522'

0   1   2

MILES

Colony Baldy
13,707'

Crestone Peak
14,294'

Crestone
Needle 14,191'

Broken Hand
Peak 13,573'

Pico Aislado
13,611'

SOUTH COLONY
Ride 41

from the right, is popular with climbers. Stash the bikes and hike up through the designated wilderness area to South Colony Lakes. Keep an eye on the weather because the bouncy ride down alone can numb the arms and take longer than it seems.

Land status: San Isabel National Forest and private holdings.

Maps: San Isabel National Forest; USGS Crestone Peak, Beck Mountain.

Access: From Westcliffe, drive 4.5 miles south on Colorado Highway 69 to County Road 119 and turn right. Drive another 5.5 miles and turn right onto CR 120. Go up about 1 mile to the parking area. If you have a four-wheel-drive you can drive up farther. But don't park on any private land. The odometer readings start at the cattle guard.

The ride:

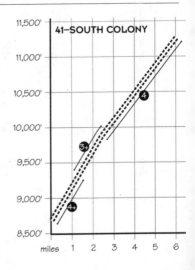

- **0.0** Head up South Colony Road (CR 120).
- **1.0** The tread becomes noticeably better.
- **1.8** National forest boundary.
- **2.4** Stay on the road as it crosses the Rainbow Trail (see Ride 42).
- **2.8** Cross South Colony Creek.
- **4.7** Cross the creek again.

6.0 The South Colony Trail passes by on the right. This is one of two ways hikers or equestrians can travel to view the lakes.

6.4 After crossing the creek the trail ends at a gate. Stash your bike here and continue—ON FOOT—straight to see the lakes.

Rainbow Trail

Location: West of Westcliffe.

Distance: 32 miles one way.

Time: 5 hours.

Tread: 30.6 miles of singletrack and 1.4 miles of dirt road. This is prime trail!

Aerobic level: Variable. Moderate to strenuous depending on distance and direction ridden.

Technical difficulty: 3+. The trail is occasionally narrow and has some rock and root obstacles.

Highlights: One of the best rides in the state! The route rolls up and down along the Sangre de Cristo Mountains without much altitude gain. Several access points allow long or short rides and two vehicles makes shuttle rides an option. The views of the Wet Mountain Valley are grand and the up-close look at the mountains is inspirational.

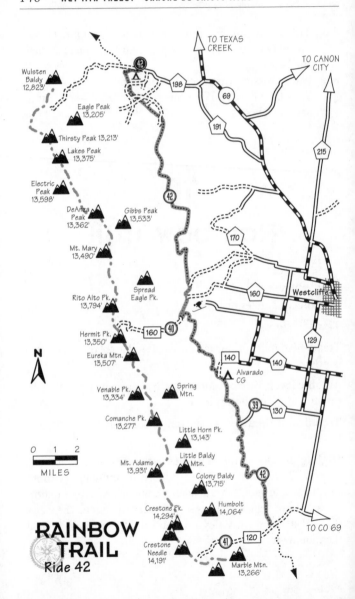

TO TEXAS CREEK

TO CANON CITY

Wulsten Baldy 12,823'

Eagle Peak 13,205'

Thirsty Peak 13,213'

Lakes Peak 13,375'

Electric Peak 13,598'

DeAnza Peak 13,362'

Gibbs Peak 13,533'

Mt. Mary 13,490'

Spread Eagle Pk.

Rito Alto Pk. 13,794'

Hermit Pk. 13,350'

Eureka Mtn. 13,507'

Westcliffe

Alvarado CG

N

Venable Pk. 13,334'

Spring Mtn.

Comanche Pk. 13,277'

Little Horn Pk. 13,143'

0 1 2
MILES

Mt. Adams 13,931'

Little Baldy Mtn.

Colony Baldy 13,715'

Crestone Pk. 14,294'

Humbolt 14,064'

TO CO 69

RAINBOW TRAIL
Ride 42

Crestone Needle 14,191'

Marble Mtn. 13,266'

Land status: San Isabel National Forest and private holdings.

Maps: San Isabel National Forest; USGS Electric Peak, Beckwith Mountain, Horn Peak, and Beck Mountain.

Access: Rides 39, 40, and 41 all list possible access points. The ride description given here starts at Lake Creek Campground. From Westcliffe drive 11 miles north on Colorado Highway 69 to County Road 198 and turn left. This dirt road turns toward the mountains and runs into the campground. Incidentally, the road turns into a four-wheel-drive road and leads to Balman Reservoir and Rainbow Lake. Four-wheelers can also access Forest Road 337, FR 332, and FR 331 to get to the trail.

The ride:

- **0.0** The well-signed Rainbow Trail access path leaves the west side of the campground.
- **0.6** Turn left onto the Rainbow Trail proper. Going right the trail runs about 20 miles to Salida!
- **1.4** Remain on the trail where it crosses FR 337.
- **2.0** Ditto. Again, remain on the trail across FR 337, followed by FR 332 and FR 338. Stay on the trail throughout.

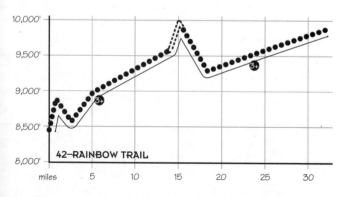

2.4 Keep left and pass by the upper trailhead for Brush Lake.

5.3 Keep left and pass by the lower trailhead for Brush Lake.

13.0 Turn right on FR 173 and continue up the road. Left leads to Westcliffe.

13.4 Turn left onto the Rainbow Trail. Again, it is well signed.

14.0 Turn right onto Hermit Lake Road (FR 160). Left here leads to Westcliffe.

15.0 Turn left onto the Rainbow Trail. A sign warning "Some roads closed due to..." marks the turn. Cross the bridge and regain the trail proper.

18.3 Keep right as the Alvarado Campground trailhead is down to the left.

23.6 Horn Creek access point passes by on the left.

32.1 South Colony Road. Turn left to return to Westcliffe or keep riding. The trail ends at Music Pass, but the description stops here.

Appendix A:

Additional Ride Information for Colorado Springs

Colorado Springs has a wide variety of city trails available. Palmer Park's terrain offers technical and aerobic challenges. While the city park and recreation department can offer information, the local bike shops remain the best source for these trails. Their fingers are on the pulse of the local fat-tire community.

Garden of the Gods features some fabulous rides amidst its world famous rock formations. The Visitor Center offers a map that shows trails and their current status. They've only recently let bikes back onto the trails. Be sure to obey all postings!

The country north of town is starting to become popular to bikers. One trail encircles Mount Herman near Monument. Exit Interstate 25 at Monument and take Mount Herman Road out of town. The trailhead is where Sunburst Road comes in.

Another popular trail runs along I-25 and the old Sante Fe Trail. Enter the south gate at the U.S. Air Force Academy and turn left onto Pine Drive. After 0.5 mile turn left onto a dirt road. The trailhead starts just over the railroad tracks.

WOODLAND PARK - DIVIDE

The Manitou Park Bike Trail lies north of Woodland Park on Colorado Highway 67 as do a variety of Forest Service Roads. These are accessible at the numerous campgrounds. Deckers, a small town to the north, has some good trails. Woodland Park bike shops should be able to give you the latest information. The Pike National Forest Map also will help. If you venture into the wilderness areas, go on foot and leave your wheels at the boundary.

OTHER REGIONS

Other local regions also have more trails to offer. Finding out about them is a word-of-mouth matter. Again, the bike shops will be the best bet. No other guide books have addressed the entire region. However, a San Isabel Map will help the adventurous find new rides.

The San Carlos Ranger District office is located in Canon City and has a wealth of information. Get the latest on the region's constantly fluctuating regulations and new trails.

For information on biking in other parts of Colorado look for Fat Trax guides to Durango, Boulder, and the Aspen-Crested Butte area. The Colorado edition of *America by Mountain Bike* is a good starting point for exploring the rest of the state.

Appendix B:
Information Sources

**USDA FOREST SERVICE
OFFICES**

**Pikes Peak Ranger District-
Pike National Forest**
601 S. Weber Street
Colorado Springs, CO 80903
(719) 636-1602

**San Carlos Ranger District - San
Isabel National Forest**
326 Dozier Avenue
Canon City, CO 81212
(719) 275-4119

OTHER FEDERAL OFFICES

Colorado State BLM Office
2850 Youngfield Street
Lakewood, CO 80215
(303) 239-3600

**United States Air Force
Academy**
2346 Academy Drive
USAF Academy
Colorado Springs, CO
80840-9400
(719) 472-1818

STATE AND LOCAL AGENCIES

Colorado Division of Wildlife
6060 Broadway
Denver, CO 80216
(303) 297-1192

**Colorado Springs Park and
Recreation Department**
1401 Recreation Way
Colorado Springs, CO 80905

General Information:
(719) 578-6640

Garden Of The Gods Park:
(719) 578-6939

**Colorado Springs
Department of Utilities**
(to get permit allowing completion of Ride 10)
(719) 636-5616

**Woodland Park Chamber
of Commerce**
P.O. Box 9022
Woodland Park, CO 80866
(719) 687-9885

**Pikes Peak Highway
Superintendent**
Cascade, CO 80809
(719) 684-9138
Tollgate: (719) 684-9383

Mueller State Park
21045 Highway 67
Divide, CO 80814
(719) 687-2366

Glossary

ATB: All-terrain bicycle; a.k.a. mountain bike, sprocket rocket, fat tire flyer.

ATV: All-terrain vehicle; in this book ATV refers to motorbikes and three- and four-wheelers designed for off-road use.

Bail: Getting off the bike, usually in a hurry, and whether or not you meant to. Often a last resort.

Bunny hop: Leaping up, while riding, and lifting both wheels off the ground to jump over an obstacle (or for sheer joy).

Clean: To ride without touching a foot (or other body part) to the ground; to ride a tough section successfully.

Clipless: A type of pedal with a binding that accepts a matching cleat on the sole of a bike shoe. The cleat locks to the pedal for more control and efficient pedaling, and is easily unlatched safe landings (in theory).

Contour: A line on a topographic map showing a continuous elevation level over uneven ground. Also a verb indicating a fairly easy or moderate grade: "The trail contours around the west flank of the mountain before the final grunt to the top."

Dab: To put a foot or hand down (or hold onto or lean on a tree or other support) while riding. If you have to dab, then you haven't ridden that piece of trail **clean.**

Downfall: Trees that have fallen across the trail.

Doubletrack: A trail, jeep road, ATV route, or other track with two distinct ribbons of **tread,** typically with grass growing in between. No matter which side you choose, the other rut always looks smoother.

Endo: Lifting the rear wheel off the ground and riding (or abruptly not riding) on the front wheel only. Also known, at varying degrees of control and finality, as a nose wheelie, "going over the handlebars," and a face plant.

Fall line: The **line** you follow when gravity is in control and you aren't.

Graded: When a gravel road is scraped level to smooth out the washboards and potholes, it has been graded. In this book, a road is listed as graded only if it is regularly maintained. Even these roads are not always graded every year.

Granny gear: The innermost and smallest of the chainrings on the bottom bracket spindle (where the pedals and crank arms attach to the bike's frame). Shift down to your granny gear (and up to the biggest cog on the rear hub) to find your lowest ratio for easiest climbing.

Hammer: To ride hard; derived from how it feels afterward: "I'm hammered."

Hammerhead: Someone who actually enjoys feeling **hammered.** A Type A rider who goes hard and fast all the time.

Line: The route (or trajectory) between or over obstacles or through turns. **Tread** or trail refers to the ground you're riding on; the line is the path you choose within the tread (and exists mostly in the eye of the beholder).

Off-the-seat: Moving your butt behind the bike seat and over the rear tire; used for control on extremely steep descents. This position increases braking power, helps prevent **endos,** and reduces skidding.

Portage: To carry the bike, usually up a steep hill, across unrideable obstacles, or through a stream.

Quads: Thigh muscles (short for quadraceps); or maps in the USGS topographic series (short for quadrangles). The right quads (of either kind) can prevent or get you out of trouble in the backcountry.

Ratcheting: Also known as backpedaling; pedaling backwards to avoid bashing feet or pedals on rocks or other obstacles.

Sidehill: Where the trail crosses a slope's **fall line**. If the **tread** is narrow, keep your uphill pedal up to avoid hitting the ground. If the tread has a sideways slant, you may have to use body English to keep the bike vertical and avoid side-slipping.

Singletrack: A trail, game run, or other track with only one ribbon of **tread.** But this is like defining an orgasm as a muscle cramp. Good singletrack is pure fun.

Spur: A side road or trail that splits off from the main route.

Surf: Riding through loose gravel or sand, when the wheels slalom from side to side. Also *heavy surf:* frequent and difficult obstacles.

Suspension: A bike with front suspension has a shock-absorbing fork or stem. Rear suspension absorbs shock between the rear wheel and frame. A bike with both is said to be fully suspended.

Switchbacks: When a trail goes up a steep slope, it zig zags or switchbacks across the **fall line** to ease the gradient of the climb. Well-designed switchbacks make a turn with at least an 8-foot radius and remain fairly level within the turn itself. These are rare, however, and cyclists often struggle to ride through sharply angled, sloping switchbacks.

Track stand: Balancing on a bike in one place, without rolling forward appreciably. Cock the front wheel to one side and bring that pedal up to the 1 or 2 o'clock position. Now control your side-to-side balance by applying pressure on the pedals and brakes and changing the angle of the front wheel, as needed. It takes practice but really comes in handy at stoplights, on **switchbacks,** and when trying to free a foot before falling. (See **clipless**)

Tread: The riding surface, particularly regarding **singletrack.**

Water bar: A log, rock, conveyor belting, ditch, or other barrier placed in the **tread** to divert water off the trail and prevent erosion. Peeled logs can be slippery and cause bad falls, especially when they angle sharply across the trail.

Whoop-te-doo: An abrupt mound of dirt across the road or trail. These are common on old logging roads and skidder tracks, placed there to block vehicle access. At high speeds, they become launching pads that transform bikes into spaceships and riders into astronauts.

A Short Index of Rides

Road Rides
(may include jeep tracks and unmaintained routes)

Sweet Singletrack Rides
(may also include road and doubletrack portions)

Beginner's Luck

28 Skyline Drive (1)
35 Junkins Park Loop (2)
36 Ghost Town Loop (2)
37 Lake DeWeese Loop (2)
38 Silver Streak (2)

Technical Tests

9 Intemann Memorial Trail (4)
15 Falcon Trail (4)
26 Tanner-Stultz Loop (5+)
31 St. Charles Peak (4+)
33 Second Mace-Dome Rock (4+)

Great Climbs—the Yearn to Burn

2 Gold Camp Road (2+)
5 St. Mary's Falls (4)
7 The Chutes (3)
10 Mount Baldy (2+)
12 Barr Trail (4-)
13 Barr-Ute Trail Loop (4-)
23 Pancake Rocks (3+)
25 Oak Creek Loop (3+)
26 Tanner-Stultz Loop (5+)
29 Snowslide Trail (4)
31 St. Charles Peak (4+)
34 Deer Peak (4+)
40 Hermit Pass (4)
41 South Colony (4)

Great Downhills—the Need for Speed

1 Captain Jack's (3-)
4 Bear Creek Loop (3+)
7 The Chutes (3)
11 Jones's Downhill (3+)
14 Elk Park-Severy Downhill (4)
25 Oak Creek Loop (3+)
32 Squirrel Creek (4)

About the Author

Hmm...what do you want to know about me?

I've loved the outdoors for as long as I can remember. I hiked, fished, spelunked, and rode while growing up in the Wet Mountain Valley.

Mountain biking as such didn't exist back then. We'd con a parent into shuttling our BMX bikes up to Alvarado campground (see Ride 39) and then ride around and bomb back to Westcliffe. I inherited a 10-speed from my brother and began riding around the old mining roads (see rides 36, 37, 38). That poor bike!

Biking took a backseat while I went to Colorado State University and still hadn't resurfaced during my "professional" career. In Summit County, Colorado, while ski-bumming, my biking passion was re-kindled. But, that's in my Acknowledgments.

Anyway, that's my mountain biking background.

Professionally I wear many hats. Photographer and writer are the most recent. I've been a private investigator, counseled behaviorally disturbed adolescents, and been a salesman for a variety of things. My official education got me a Bachelor of Science degree in Psychology.

I am currently on hiatus, taking a break from Colorado. I've lived in the state since 1976 and treasure it! But I need something to compare it to. As we go to press, I'm learning to surf in California.

I guess the main thing to know about me is that I enjoy life.

I hope this guide increases your enjoyment.

Dave

FALCON GUIDES

Get Ready to Crank

fat/trax
fat/trax Bozeman
fat/trax Colorado Springs

Dennis Coello's America By Moutain Bike Series
Mountain Biking Arizona
Mountain Biker's Guide to Central Appalachia
Mountain Biker's Guide to Colorado
Mountain Biking the Great Lake States
Mountain Biking the Great Plains States
Mountain Biking the Midwest
Mountain Biker's Guide to New Mexico
Mountain Biker's Guide to
    Northern California/Nevada
Mountain Biking Northern New England
Mountain Biker's Guide to Ozarks
Mountain Biking the Pacific Northwest
Mountain Biking the Southeast
Mountain Biker's Guide to Southern California
Mountain Biker's Guide to Southern New England
Mountain Biking Texas and Oklahoma
Mountain Biker's Guide to Utah
Mountain Biker's Guide to the Midwest

■ *To order any of these books, or to request an expanded list of available titles, please call 1-800-582-2665, or write to Falcon, PO Box 1718, Helena, MT 59624.*